A GUIDE TO
ACADEMIC PROTOCOL

A GUIDE TO ACADEMIC PROTOCOL

Mary Kemper Gunn

COLUMBIA UNIVERSITY PRESS
New York

ISBN 0-231-03036-3

Copyright © 1969 Columbia University Press

Library of Congress Catalog Card Number: 70-76250

Printed in the United States of America

10 9 8 7 6 5 4 3

To Mrs. Grayson Kirk, one of the great hostesses, whose
ability to put her guests at ease transcends mere social know-
how and stems from genuine kindness and enjoyment of
people, whether they are heads of state or foreign exchange
students, Nobel laureates or freshmen.

the old hands at other institutions, although it is addressed primarily to those people on the newer campuses who are learning to cope with the preparations for public ceremonies. Let the new people, wherever they are, proceed with confidence. As the Dean of the College at Columbia has said: "Do something for the first time and that's innovation. Thereafter it is tradition."

MARY KEMPER GUNN

October, 1968

PREFACE

ON THE ADMINISTRATIVE staff of every university, college, and similar institution there is (or should be) someone who is responsible for putting the institution's best foot forward on public occasions. Among these are receptions, lectures, dinners, convocations, the annual commencement, and the infrequent installation of a new president. On some campuses there is no central office for such work—which suffers accordingly. No person with other primary responsibilities should undertake to manage one of these public occasions with one hand while coping with his or her regular duties with the other. As I hope this book will make clear, the work can be organized in such a way that it runs smoothly and redounds to the glory of the institution, provided there is one central office handling it.

At Columbia University, as an assistant to the Secretary, I became the first such person in 1963. It was most satisfying and interesting work. I hope this book will aid and comfort

CONTENTS

Preface, vii

Introduction, 1

1. Receptions and Teas, 4
2. Lectures, 20
3. Dinners, 32
4. Church Ceremonies, 43
5. Convocations, 47
6. Commencement, 63
7. Inauguration Ceremonies, 86
8. Proper Dress for Public Occasions, 102

Appendix: Budgets and Check List, 107

A GUIDE TO
ACADEMIC PROTOCOL

Introduction: GENERAL ADVICE
TO THE NEOPHYTES

AS YOU WILL SEE in the following pages, the
key to your job, whatever its title, is meticulous attention to
detail. Just as important, however, is public relations—or,
to avoid an odious phrase, relations with the public. The
kind of impression made on a visitor to any institution depends on little courtesies and can be altered for better or
worse by the manner in which he is greeted and the type of
services rendered to him.

To do your job efficiently, it is important to establish a
schedule which is workable for your staff and facilities, and
which, if possible, becomes immutable. If not, there will
always be a department or school which expects you to arrange for an occasion with inadequate time to do a finished
job. ("But you always manage so beautifully," is the usual
gambit.) Following is the *minimum* time, in my experience, to prepare for each category of event:

Receptions and teas   6 weeks
Dinners   7 weeks

Lectures	2 months
Convocations	3 months
Commencement	4 months
Installation	6 months (a year would be better)

This schedule is based on the average time it takes the printing office on most campuses to process copy: approximately two weeks.

At Columbia, invitations to anything are generally mailed three weeks before the event. The collecting of names and addresses of guests should be begun at the same time as the printing of invitations, that is, six weeks before the event, if you feel the campus printing services will honor your request within two weeks of submitting copy. You will then have a week to cross-check the various lists (from the hostess, the school involved, the President's office, the guest of honor, and so forth) to avoid duplications and to make up a card file of those invited before addressing envelopes.

Before doing anything toward an event, it is wise to check, on-campus and off-campus as well, to see if there is something else planned for that date which would conflict. If there is no clearinghouse of such information on the campus, do your best to inaugurate one—in your own office as a last resort. The extra work entailed will pay off in the long run in better attendance at each ceremony and in improved public relations.

Everything about the work becomes easier if you make a check list for each event. You will find at the end of each section of this book a suggested list of chores to be done. It is advisable to make up a master check list which covers all possible services for any occasion, and to have it mimeographed. Start a new one for each event. You can then tell at a glance the progress of the work, and can report to your superior where matters stand on any given day. This looks efficient, by and large is, and will allow you to sleep at night in the comforting conviction that nothing has been overlooked.

One last word in general: your most valuable asset is the appearance of calmness no matter what beyond your control may go wrong at the last moment. You can give confidence to a faculty wife whose turn it is to be hostess for the first time at a large gathering, or take some of the load off the shoulders of overburdened administration wives if these people are sure you know what you are doing. Of course, just as our forefathers sought freedom only to *pursue* happiness, the best you can hope for, if some sudden catastrophe looms, is to *appear* calm. This often has an analgesic effect on *you* as well as on the other participants, and a solution presents itself quickly.

Finally, remember that your work is largely finished *before* the event, and is "underground," so to speak. To the assembled guests the ceremony or party should appear to be solely the accomplishment of the host or hostess. You will probably attend, to keep a quiet eye on ushers or waiters, but you must attempt to look like a guest, not the stage manager.

So much for the rationale. Now to get down to specifics.

1 RECEPTIONS AND TEAS

RECEPTIONS and teas serve the purpose of gathering together a large number of persons to mark an occasion. They are the backbone of academic entertaining, first of all because a great many people can be accommodated by them, and second because they are less expensive than other social functions. Nothing is watched more carefully in a university than the almighty budget.

There are, of course, many kinds of receptions and teas. To treat receptions first, there are those held before or following an important event; receptions that are intramural, such as those for freshmen or new faculty; or receptions mainly for the noncampus-based public, such as one to unveil a new exhibition of paintings or sculpture, or to honor an eminent campus visitor. They may take place either in the afternoon or evening.

In planning a reception the following determinants must be settled:

> Place and time
> Guest list and invitations

Decorations and music
Reception line members
    (announced or not)
    (auxiliary hosts and hostesses or not)
Food and drink

PLACE AND TIME

Before the place for a reception can be determined, it is necessary to decide its purpose and approximately how many people will attend. If the committee in charge (there usually is one) has records of previous similar occasions, this will be a guideline. The time of year, the weather that can be expected, the importance of the occasion, whether anything else is booked for the same date—all of these are possible factors in arriving at a working attendance figure. (Sometimes you may wish for a crystal ball.)

Arriving at an educated guess at the early stage of planning is necessary because if there is a choice of space in which to hold the reception, it must be made at the beginning. A good rule of thumb for a stand-up party is to allow a minimum of four square feet of usable floor space per person expected. Any less is uncomfortable, and the noise level becomes unpleasant no matter how good the acoustics of the room. On the other side of the picture, do not invite so few people nor use so large a reception room that there are more than eight square feet per guest, or the room will look empty. This space allotment is, of course, *usable* floor space. Room must be allowed for the serving tables and the reception line, with ample space to move around them also. For example, suppose there are to be two buffet tables about 18 feet long. Allow 90 square feet for each. If there are to be six persons in the receiving line, allow 60 square feet there. Then suppose you are using a room which measures 40 by 60, or 2,400 square feet. Subtracting the allowance for tables and receiving line (240 feet) from 2,400, there will be 2,160 square feet for guests. Divide this figure by 4 and there will be space to accommodate 540 people at a maximum. If less than 300 are expected, hold the reception in a smaller room.

The time for the reception, of course, has to be decided upon by the hostess and sometimes the dean of a school involved. It is the feeling at Columbia that for an afternoon reception the time span, if stated on the invitation, should not exceed two hours, so that those attending will not straggle in over a long period of time but will arrive within an hour of each other and leave nearly together. (Remember, the reception line people have *feet* which can hurt just like yours or mine.) For an evening reception the time span can be three hours as it is expected to fill the evening.

GUEST LIST AND INVITATIONS

At most institutions there is a department of Central Records, or its equivalent, which contains addressograph lists of faculty, administration officials, office personnel, and so forth. For each person there should be two separate addresses, office and home. If your guest list contains one or more of these categories, the envelopes may be addressed by the addressograph service, or a flat list made of those you plan to invite from which you hand-address the envelopes. You will seldom use the office address because nearly all of the ceremonies covered in this book are social and should include the wives or husbands, as the case may be. The addressograph home addresses should include spouses when they exist. There is no community more uxorious than the university. Leave a wife out at your peril.

If the reception or tea in question is for off-campus people, the hostess will probably be the best source for the addresses. It is important to get a fair idea of how many people will be invited as early as possible, because on the number of guests expected depends much that must be done at the outset: choosing a room, ordering the invitations, arranging for the food, and so on.

There are several kinds of invitations which are appropriate for receptions, some formal and some informal. The choice is dictated by the solemnity of the event and its importance on the university calendar.

The most formal is the engraved invitation, but it is the least often used. The stock for such invitations should be a very heavy vellum card, with matching envelopes of a lighter gauge. Because engraving is expensive, involving the making of a plate, it is perfectly acceptable to leave blank spaces to be filled in by hand, so that the plate can be used over and over again. Thus:

The President of Ivy University
and
Mrs. John Brown
request the pleasure of your company

at

on

at   *o'clock*

at

Please reply to

Room 213 Addison Memorial Library

After the first "at" write in "a reception for new faculty" or "a reception to honor so-and-so" or "a reception following Commencement." At line six, after "on," the date should be written out, e.g., "November seventeenth." At line seven, following "at," write out the time, e.g., "five." For the eighth line, write out the place where the reception will be held, e.g., "The Faculty Club." "Please reply to" can, of course, be "R.s.v.p.," and the address under that should be the office of whoever is keeping the list of acceptances.

If the occasion is slightly less formal, or if the invitation list exceeds the number that can practicably be filled in by hand, then the invitations will be entirely printed. There are a number of kinds of printing styles that can be used, those with raised type, which to the untutored eye look and feel engraved, and those which are frankly printed. At Columbia we lean toward the latter, as there are many well-designed typefaces which can present an attractive and dignified appearance and are not masquerading as something they are not, namely engraved.

If printed, the invitation will contain all of the information of the finished engraved invitation, that is, what was engraved and what was added by hand.

THE PRESIDENT OF IVY UNIVERSITY

AND

MRS. JOHN BROWN

REQUEST THE PLEASURE OF YOUR COMPANY

AT A RECEPTION TO HONOR

DR. WILLIAM JONES

ON NOVEMBER EIGHTEENTH

NINETEEN HUNDRED AND SIXTY-NINE

AT EIGHT O'CLOCK IN THE EVENING

AT THE FACULTY CLUB

Please reply to
213 Addison Memorial Library   *Black tie*

A reply card and addressed envelope may be enclosed with the invitation, but it is not generally done unless there is a need to send tickets of admission to those who accept.

The proper reply to such an invitation should be written on small note paper, or what are called "informals," which are a fold about three by four inches on the face of which is engraved either "Mr. and Mrs. So-and-So" or merely "Mrs. So-and-So." (No initials. The full name must be spelled out.) Inside the fold, the following should be handwritten:

> *Mr. and Mrs. So-and-So accept with pleasure*
> *the kind invitation of President and Mrs. Brown*
> *to the reception for Dr. Jones on*
> *November eighteenth at eight o'clock*
> *at the Faculty Club.*

The reason that all of the particulars of the invitation are written out is so that the hostess will be assured that her guests have noted the date, time, and place correctly.

If you cannot attend, the formula varies only a little, thus:

> *Mr. and Mrs. So-and-So regret that they will*
> *be unable to accept the kind invitation of*
> *President and Mrs. Brown to the reception*
> *for Dr. Jones on November eighteenth.*

In this case you do not need to add time and place. No reason need be given for not attending, although there seems to be a growing inclination to add to the formula a sentence such as: "They will be out of the country," or "due to unavoidable circumstances," or simply, "They will be sorry to miss it."

DECORATIONS AND MUSIC

The decorations will, of course, be dictated by the room to be used. If it is a large empty hall, more rather than less decorations are called for. Here are some suggestions: large bunches of greens—rhododendron is useful—in the corners of the room; two big potted plants rented for the occasion from a florist, placed on either side of the receiving line; large floral arrangements in the center of each buffet table, which can be elevated on boxes masked with a cloth; and tall candelabra on either side of the flowers. The buffet tables can also have a garland of greens looped along their front faces or fern leaves laid on the table itself. Try to avoid a funeral parlor aspect, which too much green and blossoms can achieve.

Music, if the reception exceeds three hundred persons, adds a festive air in a large room. It should not dominate at any time and should be chosen in accordance with the probable taste of the guests. For instance, for freshmen, a small student jazz group; for new faculty, the music department's best string quartet; for the outside public, either the string quartet or a professional group from a local hotel which can play the "potted palm" type of music—show tunes, Latin rhythms, and waltzes—politely. If your budget does not allow for "live" music, your audio-visual department can probably set up a record- or tape-playing machine in a corner of the room, but it is not by any means as festive as live music, and someone will have to spend hours choosing appropriate recorded selections.

RECEPTION LINE MEMBERS

Ideally the reception line should consist of no more than six people, or eight at the most. The shorter the line the less bottleneck at the door. In most cases the line starts with the host and hostess, next the honored guest and his wife, and last either the dean of the school most concerned (in the case of an exhibit), or the administrative officer, such as the Provost or the Vice-President, most appropriate for the occasion, and the wife of this dean or officer. If there are others who might well be included, they may be asked to be auxiliary hosts and hostesses. For instance at a reception to welcome the freshman class, the receiving line should consist of the President and his lady, the dean of the college (if there is only one), and perhaps the senior admissions officer. Then the other admissions people with whom the freshmen presumably had their initial contact can be asked to circulate on the floor, and help the young people overcome their self-consciousness.

In any case, if there is to be a sizable guest list, an announcer should be used. This young man stands just to one side of the start of the receiving line and asks each person's name as he appears and introduces him to the first person on the line, who then passes him on giving his name to the next, and so forth. The announcer must be very quick with names and have a degree of social ease. He must also be prepared to shake hands what may seem endlessly. It is a good idea if possible to give the announcer the file of acceptances so that he can familiarize himself with the names he may be expected to pronounce. This is particularly important if you expect many from abroad.

All of the ladies on the receiving line except the hostess should wear corsages. The auxiliary hostesses should also wear a smaller version, and the gentlemen on the receiving line and those acting as hosts should have boutonnieres. This helps to distinguish them from the guests and gives them a status which they may need to mask their own lack of ease. These flowers can be ordered at the same time as the decorations.

FOOD AND DRINK

For a reception for students, you will want to serve substantial food no matter what the time of day. (It is astonishing how much they can eat in a between-meal snack. This may be a comment on the quality of food served in dormitories, but it's more likely biochemical.) Sandwiches made of roast beef, chicken, turkey, ham, or ham and cheese are by far the favorites of young people. Cookies, brownies, small iced cakes, even a few plates of candies are not amiss. None of these are beyond the capabilities of university food services, which usually cater intramural parties. If the sandwiches mentioned above are too expensive for your budget, a good chicken salad and some cheese spreads are useful, as well as combinations based on cream cheese. In any case, the sandwiches should have the crusts either removed altogether or shaved off somewhat, and the sandwiches should be cut in thirds or even fourths if the slice of bread is large. For undergraduates a minimum of three sandwiches each (before cutting) and a half-dozen cookies or cakes should be allotted (more if you can afford it; they will, like the locust, eat everything in sight).

For beverage, serve a good fruit punch, and have enough on hand to allow three glasses each. If you are also going to serve coffee, have a big bowl of whipped cream by the coffee urn instead of pitchers of cream. This adds a coffeehouse touch that young people seem to like, especially if there is some cinnamon or shaved chocolate to sprinkle on top of the dob of whipped cream floating in the coffee.

For adult guests, the fare can be a little more sophisticated. Canapes made of all the standard things are usual, and if your facilities allow it, hot canapes passed from time to time, but only if they are really hot. A few tea sandwiches—dainty bite-sized sorts—and some little iced cakes are a pleasant addition. You will find that you do not need to allow so many canapes for adults as you would for students, although we had one notable exception at Columbia when we once provided a dozen canapes for each invited guest and ran out an hour before the party was due to end. The guests were a delegation from South America, and we shall never know whether many more came than were planned for or whether they thought—what with the language barrier—that they had been invited for dinner at five in the afternoon.

For drinks at an adult reception, a fruit punch spiked with rum is good, or a domestic brand of dry sherry. In any case, a nonalcoholic punch should also be offered for those whose religion or scruples forbid alcohol.

FORMAL EVENING RECEPTIONS

Occasionally an institution will decide to hold a large evening reception to mark an event of extraordinary importance—the announcement of a new program or school, the welcome of a new president or chancellor, a visit to the campus of an internationally important figure, or the beginning of a capital fund drive. Very likely the hosts of the reception will be the President and the chairman of the trustees. In this case, the invitations will begin:

THE PRESIDENT AND THE TRUSTEES OF IVY UNIVERSITY
REQUEST THE HONOR OF YOUR PRESENCE

AT A RECEPTION TO {
COMMEMORATE
INTRODUCE
ANNOUNCE
}

etc.

The second line has more weight and solemnity than the usual "pleasure of your company." The invitation should include in the lower right-hand corner the euphemism "black tie," which indicates to both men and women guests that they should wear dinner clothes.

The reception will probably be held off-campus in a hotel ballroom or a country club or large restaurant unless there is a suitable hall on campus. This sort of gathering is usually attended by campus dignitaries, alumni association officials, representatives of the government (state and local), the clergy, donors of sizable amounts to the university, professors emeriti, presidents of neighboring institutions of higher learning, and leading businessmen from the community. In all cases the wives, when they exist, must also be invited.

There will inevitably be a committee to work with. They will be of little use in compiling the guest list, but they will choose the decorations, food, drink, music, and so forth, and they will want to confer endlessly with the maître d'hôtel or the caterer unless someone takes a firm hand at the meetings.

Here are some cautions to consider: the caterer will suggest several choices of food. The committee should choose among these and not try to give him Aunt Susie's marvelous recipe for strawberry mousse to prepare. He knows what he can do best within the limitations of his kitchen and staff. If you ask for something he has not served before you are courting disaster.

Drink should be simple and not lethal if alcohol is incorporated. A tea-based fruit punch with rum added in about one-to-four proportions will catch no one by surprise. A grander punch, but more expensive, is one part brandy, one part domestic champagne, two parts soda water, and two parts ginger ale, in which are floated strawberries or small pieces of fresh pineapple. In either case, always have at least one bowl of nonalcoholic punch for the nondrinkers.

Things to check on: parking space and parking attendants; ample checkroom facilities for both men and women; corsages for the ladies in the receiving line; a guest book near the door to be signed by all of the guests; musicians briefed to play continuously, or as nearly so as they will agree to; transportation and escort service for the guests of honor to and from the reception.

TEAS

Teas differ from receptions in that they always take place in the afternoon and are generally more informal than receptions. Invitations can be written on "informals" described above, or printed if the guest list is long, or telephoned if it is short. If the invitation is written or printed, a reply is optional, but helpful to the hostess.

There is generally no reception line at a tea. The hostess stays near the door to greet her guests and direct them to a coatroom, and she will ask some of her friends and colleagues to act as auxiliary hostesses, especially if the tea involves many newcomers to the campus.

If there are to be as many as a hundred guests, at least two serving areas or tables should be set up, with coffee and tea services at either end of each. Four experienced faculty wives should be asked to pour, and at least two maids or butlers should be on hand to replenish the supply of fresh cups, pass plates of food, and keep the coffee and tea urns filled.

The room or rooms should be decorated with greens and at least one spectacular flower arrangement, and the tea tables also should each have one large bouquet in the center flanked by candelabra, the more elaborate the better. (Here you can let yourself go on decorations. There are bound to be local garden club aficionados to notice.) The coffee and tea services should be beautifully polished silver on silver trays, and the china the best available. The tablecloths should be linen or damask, and if possible the tea napkins also, although paper napkins are now in common use.

For some reason, perhaps because they are attended almost entirely by women, the food at teas assumes more importance than at any similar gathering. There should be a great variety of dainty sandwiches in different shapes, some no larger than a silver dollar, some many-layered and elaborate. The fillings are seldom substantial, tending to salads, watercress and cream cheese, and sea food. Several varieties of cookies, brownies, and small cakes should make up about half of the foods served. Bowls of salted nuts, stuffed dates, or candies can be put on the tea tables, but these are a form of lagniappe and are not passed to the guests. No one will eat a great volume, but everyone is likely to sample each item, if only to have something to comment on to her neighbor.

If the tea is to be small enough so that everyone can sit down, then two or three beautifully iced layer cakes can be served on cake plates along with the coffee or tea. Since small teas are seldom considered "public ceremonies" they are not the concern of this book.

CHECK LIST FOR RECEPTIONS AND TEAS

Place _____

Date _____

Time _____

Host or

Hostess _____

Preparation of guest list

Lists from _____ Rec'd _____

_____   _____

_____   _____

Orders for printing

Invitations

Number _____

Delivery date _____

Mailing date _____

Reply cards and envelopes

Number _____

Delivery date_____

Envelopes
  Number_____
  Delivery date_____
  Typed_____ Addressographed_____
  Hand addressed_____
Record of mailing
  Flat list_____
  3 x 5 file cards
  Tally:_____yes_____no_____
Buildings and grounds set-up
  Checking facilities in_____   for_____ men
                                        _____women

  Matrons needed_____from____ to _____
  Tables needed_____in _____
  Janitors needed_____from____ to _____
Hired music
  Source_____ Contractor_____
  To play from_____ to_____
Flowers
  From_____
  Table arrangements_____
  Corsages_____   Boutonnieres_____
  Delivery time_____   Delivery place_____
Receiving line
  Number_____   Invited by_____
Escorts for honored guests
            _____to escort_____
            _____to escort_____
Instructions to escorts and parking attendants
  Written_____   Verbal_____

2 *LECTURES*

ENDOWED LECTURES, whether singles or series, are a large part of the extracurricular program at a university or college. The older the institution, the more such lectures are in force. At Columbia there are about twenty which are open to the university at large and in many cases to the public as well. No admission is charged for any of them. In some instances tickets are issued when the speaker is so well known that more people will want to attend than the fire laws allow. (In some cases the speaker is not so well known, and then an all-out effort must be made to attract a good-sized audience.)

The first steps in obtaining the star are undertaken by the President, or a dean, or a chairman of the committee for the lecture, who writes to invite the speaker. He outlines what the lecture's history has been, who have been the previous speakers, the fee or honorarium offered, the publishing arrangements with the university press, whether the university will pay for transportation, hotel, etc., for the lecturer and his wife, and suggests convenient dates for the appearance.

When he gets an acceptance, the original letter-writer replies expressing his pleasure, confirming the date or dates chosen, and informing the speaker that so-and-so (in Columbia's case, usually the Secretary of the university) will be in touch with him shortly about details.

The person thus designated then writes for the following information:

Date and time the lecturer will arrive
Whether or not the lecturer plans to bring his wife
The title of the lecture or lectures (for the program)
A list of people the lecturer would like to have receive invitations to attend either the lecture or the dinner
A glossy photograph for the news office

He also tells the lecturer that his reservations will be made, if he wishes, for travel and for hotel accommodations; that he will be met at the airport or station, and by whom; that he is to be given a dinner before the lecture, and that his host, from whom he will be hearing, will be so-and-so. He also makes clear whether the dinner is to be "informal" or "black tie."

After these preliminaries, the person who is in charge of details takes over. First of all is the big question: which room or hall will be used for the lecture? Provided there is a choice of appropriate places, someone has to decide how large a crowd the speaker will draw from the student body, the faculty, and the outside world. At Columbia, we seldom have this problem. University-wide lectures are usually held in the Rotunda of Low Memorial Library because it is handsome and because the number of seats is adjustable. There is a dais at one end of the room, and the floor can hold as few as 400 chairs without looking bare, yet has the capacity for 750. Therefore our only problem has been to estimate how many chairs to bring in.

It is surprising how wrong a guess may be. For instance, one of the former shining lights of Columbia's faculty was recently invited to return to give an endowed lecture. He had been a brilliant and popular teacher, so naturally we expected a full house, mostly students. As it turned out, the auditorium was about half-full. We had overlooked the fact that the upper classmen and graduate students of two years before were gone, and none of the current student body had ever had a class with this man. The audience consisted of his former colleagues and a handful of people who had read his books. Because the Rotunda was the site of the lecture, however, it was possible to take down some of the chairs which, it was apparent fifteen minutes before the scheduled starting time, would clearly not be needed, so at least the lecturer was not confronted with an acre of empty seats.

Of course, the opposite can also occur. A few years ago, a Canadian scholar was invited to give a series of four lectures on, as I remember, "The Romance of Shakespeare." I was told that he was an eminent Shakespearean scholar, but no one would hazard a guess as to his drawing power. To play it safe, 400 chairs were set up and an additional 100 stacked near at hand in case they were needed. I think we had to put up a few of the extras the first night. This opening lecture was as brilliant, witty, and enlightening as any we had had that year. As well, it was rather outspoken when dealing with the "romance" of Falstaff and Doll Tearsheet and some others. As it happened there were two nuns in the audience, and I hoped that they were not affronted.

The second lecture, which occurred the following night, brought out an audience of about 650, or at least a fifty per cent increase. The successive lectures filled the hall to capacity. Fortunately we were prepared for them. What I will never understand, however, is that the second night there were not two but six nuns present, and at the final two lectures, twelve nuns at each. One can only presume that the ladies decided to overlook the earthiness of the lecturer's comments in order to benefit from his insights.

A third and disastrous situation which can occur and over which there is no control took place at a sister institution a few years ago. A world-famous poet and critic was triumphantly captured to deliver a series of lectures as one of his rare public appearances. It was scheduled for the largest lecture hall on campus. Every seat was filled and all of the standing room taken, and still they came. Students crowded the windows, and an air of barely suppressed exaltation awaited the Great Man. In due course he arrived, was introduced by an important dean, and began. Horror of horrors, his platform presence was incredibly bad. Although American-born, he had acquired all of the worst Colonel Blimpisms of the British. He mumbled, stuttered, lost his place in his notes, and finally settled for reading the lecture, pages held six inches from his nose, in a monotonous drone.

The faces at the windows soon disappeared, the standees began to thin, and the captive seated audience twitched and fidgeted audibly. When the lecture mercifully came to an end, the applause was only polite. My alter ego on that campus hastily switched the next lecture to a much smaller auditorium, being unable to cancel it altogether, and even there the audience had dwindled to a large handful. The final lecture was held in a master's study, attended by the loyal few English majors who persisted in believing that the Great Man would drop some pearls of wisdom. They were amply rewarded. In the informal atmosphere he flowered, was witty and profound, encouraged open discussion, and answered questions freely. Fortunately the session was tape-recorded and is still played on that campus for students of the man's work. The difficulty, of course, had been that he was painfully shy, and the sight of a thousand faces staring back at him at the first lecture had reduced him to jelly, so that he was compelled to hide behind his lecture notes.

I regret to say, there's nothing that can be done about such an incident, except to hope it doesn't occur.

PREPARATIONS

When all of the information necessary for the work has been gathered, the mechanics are much the same as for a reception—that is, the preparation of copy for invitations, reply cards, tickets (if used), programs, and so forth for the printers. The invitation lists are assembled at the same time. The type of lecture and the department in charge of it dictate whether the invitation list includes people from off-campus mainly, faculty and students of a particular discipline, or a judicious mixture of them all. No two lectures are exactly alike in their potential audience.

The copy for the printer can also vary considerably. It can read:

THE PRESIDENT OF

IVY UNIVERSITY

TAKES PLEASURE IN INVITING YOU

TO ATTEND

THE EIGHTEENTH ANNUAL CALIBER LECTURES

DECEMBER 4, 5, 9, and 10, 1969

AT EIGHT-THIRTY IN THE EVENING

THE ADDISON MEMORIAL HALL

THE CALIBER LECTURER FOR 1969 IS

DR. JOSEPH JOHN JONES

WHO WILL SPEAK ON

"THE HEBRIDES POETS"

Please reply on	*Cards of admission*
the enclosed card	*will be sent*
by December first	*upon request*

As this is a series, it is easier for the recipient of the invitation to have the dates given in numbers, as above.

On the third page of the invitation should be listed the individual titles of the four lectures under the date of each. A reply card and envelope should be enclosed which lists only the four dates thus:

Please send   tickets for the Caliber Lectures
on the following dates:
Thursday, December 4———— Tuesday, December 9————
Friday, December 5————Wednesday, December 10————

Name_____
        (please print)

Address_____Zip code_____

On the second page of the invitation, a short biography of
the lecturer can appear, as well as a short history of the lecture series; and on the fourth (back) page of the invitation,
a list of the previous "Caliber" lecturers and the overall
title of their lectures can be listed.

The foregoing is the most elaborate invitation used. It
can also double as a program to be handed out at the door.

A simpler version of a single lecture follows:

THE PRESIDENT OF IVY UNIVERSITY
AND
THE DEAN OF THE SCHOOL OF INTERNATIONAL AFFAIRS
ARE PLEASED TO ANNOUNCE A LECTURE IN THE
JOHN DOE MEMORIAL LECTURE SERIES
TO BE DELIVERED BY
THE HONORABLE SIR MAGNUS CHARTERIS
ON THE TOPIC
"RUNYMEDES: THEN AND NOW"
THURSDAY, APRIL THIRD, NINETEEN SIXTY-NINE
AT EIGHT-THIRTY IN THE EVENING
ADDISON MEMORIAL HALL

In this case, no ticket is required, and so no reply card is
necessary. It is important, however, to have posters made

which clearly state that no ticket is required, so that students will be encouraged to attend.

This latter version of "announcing" a lecture is rather chancy if there is danger that your speaker is not well-known or his speech is of narrow interest. The important thing is to fill the hall with a respectable number of people, and if there is no way to measure interest, such as through ticket requests, then there must be supplementary means of drumming up an audience. One is to ask faculty members with classes in the discipline of the lecture to encourage their students to attend; another is to get the student paper to run a story on the lecturer; another is to send the announcement to all of the faculty widows in the area. They are a stalwart group who, in all sorts of weather, will turn out for almost anything if bid, bless them.

Now that you have the invitations under control, the remaining chores can best be followed up through your check list. For instance, as soon as you have the reply from the lecturer about his arrival and so forth, make his *reservation* both for travel and for hotel. Arrange for someone to meet him at his point of arrival.

If he is not an American, clear with your superior whether to order the *flag* of his country placed beside the American flag on the lecture platform. (If so, facing the stage, the American flag is always on the left and that of another nation on the right.)

Send the orders to Buildings and Grounds and the Security Department, or whatever they are called on your campus. Find out from the person in charge of the lecture who is to introduce whom so that the right number of chairs can be placed on the platform. If one of the university's top echelon is to present the lecturer, then someone a little less celestial must introduce *him*. Therefore you will need three *chairs* on the platform, and three glasses with the pitcher of water beside the lectern.

If the lecture is to be taped, send the order for the *taping* to the audio-visual department, and if the lecture is to be illustrated with slides or film, explain what equipment will be needed. You will want to engage two engineers (probably students), one to run the projector and the other to monitor the p.a. system and tape the lecture. *Slides* have a way of getting out of order or upside down quite often. This is an inexplicable phenomenon with which all lecturers are familiar, and all academic audiences as well. The p.a. system, however, can and should be in the hands of someone who knows how to anticipate or avoid the squeal of a sudden overload or drop in output. If it happens more than once, keep changing engineers until one is found who can maintain control of the fiendish mechanism, and takes pride in doing so.

Notify the *news office* of the lecture, and if there is to be a press conference, set the wheels rolling. In any case, tell the news office people when they may expect biographical material and the photograph of the lecturer.

Whatever the financial procedure at the institution, it will be necessary to order the speaker's *check* far enough in advance so that it can be given to him on the night of his lecture. If there is to be a series, the custom may be to give him half of the honorarium on the first night and the remainder on the last.

If you use student *ushers,* be sure that they report a half-hour before the lecture is to begin. Instruct them clearly about seating plans (i.e., the dinner party must be seated in a reserved section at the front of the auditorium), and emphasize the need for unflagging courtesy.

A word about *checking facilities:* they are seldom adequate at any university, because unless they were provided for when the building was erected, they must be set up in space that is invariably inadequate. At least six attendants with racks for several hundred coats should be provided if the expected attendance is over two or three hundred. Guests usually arrive for a lecture over a period of half an hour, but when the lecture is over everyone wants his coat and hat at the same time. There is no ultimate solution for this problem except the goodwill and patience of the guests.

Here is a check list for lectures, and although dinners as such are discussed in the following chapter, I have included the dinner before the lecture here, as the record of preparations for both can best be kept together.

CHECK LIST FOR LECTURES

Lecturer_____

Title _____

Place_____

Date _____

Time_____

Preparation of guest list
  Lists of _____   from _____ Rec'd_____
        _____   from _____ Rec'd_____
        _____   from _____ Rec'd_____
        _____   from _____ Rec'd_____

Orders for printing
  Invitations to lecture   Invitations to dinner
    Number_____   Number_____
    Delivery date_____   Delivery date_____
    Mailing date_____   Mailing date_____
  Reply cards and envelopes
    Number_____
    Delivery date_____
  Envelopes (outer)
    Number_____
    Delivery date_____
    Typed_____ Addressographed_____ Hand addressed ____
  Posters
    Number_____
    Delivery date_____
  Programs_____
    Number_____
    Delivery date_____
  Tickets_____
    Number_____
    Delivery date_____
  Record of mailing_____
    Flat list_____   3 x 5 file cards_____
    Acceptances, lecture_____
    Acceptances, dinner_____
Student recruiting _____
  Ushers from_____Captain_____
    Report to _____at_____

Parking attendants from_____Captain_____
Report to_____ at_____
Public address system (Visual-Aid Department)
Date ordered_____
Microphones at_____ and _____
table mike_____ lectern_____
Tape-recording of lecture_____
Slides and screen_____ size _____
Films_____ type_____
Buildings and Grounds set-up
Checking facilities in_____ for_____
Matrons needed_____from_____to _____
Chairs on dais _____
Flags: American_____   Other_____
                                       Rented from_____
No. of chairs on floor_____   in reserve_____
Janitor on duty from _____   to _____
Doors open at_____
Security
Special guards_____   Stations_____
Escort for honored guest _____
Travel arrangements
Arrival _____Date_____ Time_____
Departure_____ Date_____ Time_____
Chauffeur engaged_____-
Hotel reservations_____
Type of room_____Cost per day_____
Engaged from _____to _____
Dinner
Place _____Time_____Date_____
Number of guests_____Flowers ordered_____
Checking facilities_____Matron on duty_____
Menu ordered_____Seating lists typed _____
Escort for guest of honor _____

3   *DINNERS*

DINNERS at academic institutions follow much the same pattern as fairly formal dinners everywhere except that seating arrangements and order of precedence are somewhat different. The sort of dinner most often given at a university is one that precedes an event of importance on campus.

Let us consider a dinner before an endowed lecture. Its preparation should be started at roughly the same time that work on the lecture begins—that is, six weeks before the event. The guest of honor will be the lecturer and the dinner is to be at the Faculty Club. Let us assume that the host and hostess are to be the chairman of a department and his wife. They will compile a list of people to be invited. If the list is no longer than about forty names, the invitations should be handwritten. (Sometimes the hostess will undertake this job herself, but it is more likely that it will be given to you.) The invitations should read:

DR. [OR PROFESSOR] AND MRS. JOHN BLANCKE
REQUEST THE PLEASURE OF YOUR COMPANY
AT A DINNER TO HONOR
DR. JOSEPH JOHN JONES
ON DECEMBER FOURTH
NINETEEN HUNDRED AND SIXTY-NINE
AT SIX-THIRTY IN THE EVENING
AT THE FACULTY CLUB

R.s.v.p.
[*host's address*]   *Black tie*

If it is not to be a dress affair, then the third line should read: "at an informal dinner" and of course the words "black tie" eliminated. There is a tendency lately to write "dress optional" on such invitations but that seems to me cowardly and unfair, if not barbarous. Which does one choose in that case? And will one be with the minority or the majority, whichever is chosen?

When deciding on the time of the dinner several factors must be considered: whether or not cocktails or sherry will be served, and what time the lecture is scheduled to start. For an eight-thirty lecture, the dinner itself should begin as near seven o'clock as late arrivals allow. If cocktails are to be served, the invitation should be for six-thirty. In fact, the invitations can so read. Instead of the time being included in the body of the invitation, the schedule can appear under "black tie" in the lower right-hand corner:

Black tie
Cocktails at six-thirty
Dinner at seven

Then if there are teetotalers among the guests they need not appear until seven, and the others are put on notice that they will not get a drink if they are late.

THE SEATING PLAN

When all of the answers are in and you have the guest list established, it is better to work out a tentative seating plan in the quiet of your office and then consult with the hostess. She may want to change it all around, but you are likely to save a good deal of time, nonetheless, by having something to work with. There are, after all, certain immutable rules which need to be followed.

1. The guest of honor must be on the right hand of the hostess, and his wife on the right of the host.
2. Husbands and wives must not sit next to each other.
3. You must wherever possible alternate men and women.

Unfortunately, in the academic community it often happens that there are not an equal number of men and women on the guest list. At Columbia the lesser number is usually the women—not that Columbia faculty do not marry as relentlessly as all others, but many of them live a distance out of the city, and their wives cannot or do not always choose to come in for dinners.

The ideal seating arrangement occurs only when you have a multiple of four plus one couple, that is, eighteen, twenty-two, twenty-six, and so forth. If you work this out you will see that, alternating men and women, there needs to be an even number on each side of the host couple. If you have an extra couple, then, it is well to use an oval table and seat the host and hostess on the long sides of the oval, not at the ends. They will not be precisely opposite each other, but if the group is large enough this will not appear awkward.

   To illustrate, suppose you have an ideal number: twenty-six people including the host and hostess. They are represented by the letters "H" and "h." (Naturally the capital is the male.) The guest couples are similarly designated by capital and lower case letters, with the "A's" reserved for the guests of honor. Here is your seating plan:

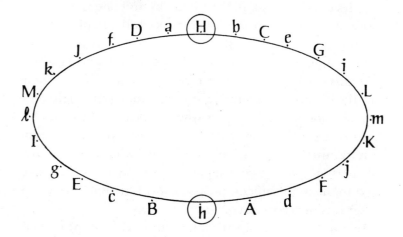

The places of honor, other than those of the A's, will be the right hand of the A's and the left hand of the H's (in this case the D's and the B's). Of secondary importance but a little above the herd would be the L's or M's, as a sort of second "head of table." You will know when you get the final guest list who should sit in these slightly elevated places.

However, there are some exceptions to note. If your D couple are dull, which is sadly sometimes the case, and you want your guests of honor to have a good time, demote the D's, to the position of L or M. They probably will be pleased. It is my observation that a dull pair are so because they do not enjoy social occasions, are ill at ease, or have no small talk. If they are seated among colleagues, they can at least talk shop.

Another exception to consider: if there are two invited couples of equal rank in the hierarchy and one is decidedly more attractive than the other, make full use of this fact. Whenever possible, put the most attractive lady next to the guest of honor. It may possibly bring on a euphoria which will affect his subsequent lecture. At the least, it will help his digestion. At Columbia there are among the higher administration several couples who are nearly indispensable for a successful dinner party. They are never at a loss for entertaining conversation no matter who their dinner partners are, and of course pay the penalty of being seated next to the most difficult people at any function, but if they suffer it is never apparent.

In the foregoing seating plan, an oval table was used. This is the usual arrangement in the private dining room at the Columbia Faculty Club, and is managed by putting together three or four rectangular tables and, at each end, half of a round table, the diameter of which is the same as the sides of the rectangular ones. They are then covered with overlapping tablecloths.

If, in making out your seating plan, you have more of one sex than the other, try to spread the wealth of the minority so that at least the most important people at the table have members of the opposite sex next to them.

When planning larger dinners than, say, for thirty-four, it is much more manageable to seat them at tables which accommodate eight or ten people. Sometimes this settles the protocol problem too. At Columbia we once had a dinner preceding the opening lecture in a science series which was attended by a most august group of guests. There were three college presidents, six deans, and seven Nobel Prize winners, as well as the heads of two foundations. There were forty-seven people in all, the rest being shining lights on the campus and distinguished research men and teachers from neighboring institutions—and of course their wives. The guest of honor wore two hats. He was a college president *and* a Nobel laureate. His wife did not come with him, nor did the wife of Dean #1. Here's a chance to test your skill in working out a seating plan. I'll give you one clue: one of the college presidents was a woman.

This is the way it worked out:

Head Table (facing forward):
  Dean #1
    Wife of Nobel #1
      Nobel #2
        Wife of Dean #2
          Foundation Head #1
            Wife of Foundation Head #2
              President of Columbia
                President of Barnard
                  Guest of Honor
                    Wife of President of Columbia
                      Foundation Head #2
                        Wife of Foundation Head #1
                          Nobel #1
                            Wife of Nobel #2
                              Dean #2

Each of four tables seating eight people was presided over by a dean and his wife. In the place of honor at each table (on the right of the dean's lady) sat a Nobel Prize winner, and where possible the others at each table had common interests, i.e., physics, biochemistry, mathematics, and so on.

This brings us to the matter of seating lists. When even your dinner party is divided among several tables, there should be a seating list available for each of the guests. If possible, make it up in two ways: alphabetically, and by table, so that each knows not only at which table he is to sit, but with whom.

Then of course, place cards must be made up and put on

the tables before the guests arrive. When writing the name —which should be beautifully lettered or written in very neat script—do not use first names: "Mrs. Jones," *not* "Mrs. John Jones," unless there are two Mrs. Joneses at the dinner. You will know the prevailing custom on your campus in regard to titles, whether your people prefer to be known as Doctor, Professor, or plain Mister. Whatever is usual, put the title and the last name on the men's cards— no first name.

MENU PLANNING

When it comes to the choice of food to be served, it is the better part of valor to let the caterer suggest three or four menus. He will list only those foods he is sure he can prepare well, and if you choose from them you are likely to arrive at the optimum he can do. There are, however, certain proscriptions you must keep in mind.

1. Serve no pork or pork products if there are Jews or Muslims in the group.
2. Serve no beef if there are Hindus.
3. It is still safer not to serve meat on Fridays to Catholics.
4. Serve nothing notably indigestible, such as lobster or corned beef.

One arrives ultimately at the only "safe" meats, which are chicken and lamb. However, Americans are predominantly beef eaters—steak and roast beef preferably. So if no Hindus have been invited, and it is not Friday, you will probably end up with one or the other. If, however, the same people attend most of the dinners at your institution, it is only merciful to vary the menu served whenever possible. For the science symposium dinner described above, the following menu was served:

Melon balls

—

Mock turtle soup

—

Roast rack of lamb
Asparagus hollandaise
Belgian carrots
Hot rolls

—

Hearts of lettuce, French dressing

—

Chocolate meringue glacé
Coffee

With a dinner of this sort it is customary, at least at eastern universities, to serve a wine with the main course, and sometimes two wines, the other with the fish if there is to be a fish course, or with the dessert. There is usually someone in the university community who is something of a wine connoisseur. He will be flattered and pleased to be consulted and to discuss what is available with the caterer or maître d'hôtel. The proper wine served at the correct temperature adds a great deal to the festive air of a formal party, and can make a good dinner seem great.

As at other social functions, decorations play a part. If the dinner is to take place in a well-appointed room, decorations other than for the table may not be necessary. If the cocktails before dinner are to be served in a different room, a handsome flower arrangement or two is probably all that is needed there. On the dining table, if the party is small enough to need only one, be sure that the candles and flowers are coordinated in color. Better a long fairly flat flower arrangement (so that people can see over them) and tall candelabra (so people can see under them). If there is to be a head table and several smaller ones, the flowers should be of the same species on all of them, and of course the candles the same color, coordinated with table linen.

It is acceptable currently to use colored tablecloths and napkins, and if the room is otherwise drab, they achieve a good effect. For instance a good combination is gold table linen, russet chrysanthemums with dark green foliage, and candles to match either the flowers or the leaves; another is light blue tablecloths, dark blue napkins, anemones or red carnations, and white candles. You might consider trying to duplicate your institution's colors in the flowers and candles, unless they are something like pomegranate and puce. Columbia's blue and white lend themselves very well to table decorations, especially in the spring when the little blue irises are available, and have been known to bring a tear to the eye of a sentimental alumnus with a well-padded checkbook.

If the dinner guests are to remain seated to hear a program of speakers, two things must be borne in mind. First, an interval between dining and listening must be provided during which the waiters may clear the tables of dessert and the ladies go to "powder their noses," and second, fresh hot coffee must be brought to the tables, along with liqueurs if they are to be served. Then, when the speeches begin, the kitchen staff must be enjoined to make no clatter which might be heard in the dining room.

When planning a large dinner or banquet, it may be that the decision is reached to hold it in a room without adequate kitchen facilities. Such is the case at Columbia, where dinners for three or four hundred guests are held in the Rotunda of Low Library. There is no kitchen in the building, no running water on the Rotunda floor, and yet our very capable caterer manages, with infra-red stoves and other devices, to serve hot things hot and cold things cold. At the height of the season, there may be as many as three such banquets in a week. It is a feat which would be rendered unnecessary by adequate facilities. New campuses please note!

4 CHURCH CEREMONIES

THE FOREGOING CHAPTERS were concerned with entertainment and social occasions on the campus—the icing on the cake, so to speak. The following chapters deal with academic ceremonies. A university can exist without the social froufrou, but its standing in the world of education and its significance as a force in the progress of the nation are celebrated by its academic ceremonies. Among these are ceremonies that are religious in character.

On most campuses church services and related activities are conducted entirely by the chaplains of the institution, quite independently of the academic or administrative arms. There are, however, two occasions when the three groups join for services. One is a Sunday set aside for remembrance of those in the academic community who died during the year, and the other is Baccalaureate Sunday, which is celebrated in connection with commencement.

COMMEMORATION SUNDAY

The chaplain's office undertakes to notify and sometimes correspond with the families of those who are to be memorialized at the service. Commemoration Sunday is a ceremony of the university family remembering all of its members who have died during the year, and is kept as nondenominational as possible.

For the service the following duties fall to administration. A letter, over the signature of the Secretary of the university, is sent to all department heads asking that someone from each department be appointed to attend the service if there has been a death among its members during the preceding year. The letter encloses the form for ordering academic dress (see page 54). When the forms are returned the robes and hoods must be ordered from the rental company. (Only women wear caps at the service.) At the same time, the Secretary inquires of the deans and the trustees whether they will attend and march in the procession.

When the answers are in, two marshals and two ushers—or two for each aisle—must be chosen from among the faculty. An adequate number of seats must be reserved in the front pews for those in the procession. The public, which usually consists of relatives of those who are being commemorated, are greeted at the door by the ushers and directed to the remaining pews.

The members of the academic procession must be robed and assembled in marching order by the marshals at least ten minutes before the service is to begin. At Columbia those who are to speak—the clergy and the Vice-President —and any trustees and deans all sit in the chancel area; the members of the faculty wearing academic dress in the front pews; the choir in its stalls.

Here is the order of the processional (which is reversed for the recessional).

Choir
Faculty (in order of rank, lowest first)
Deans
Trustees
Clergy
Vice-President

The program at Columbia consists of an invocation, Bible readings by chaplains of the three major faiths, an anthem by the choir, a sermon and a reading of the roll of honor by the Vice-President, benediction by the senior chaplain, and the recessional hymn.

It is necessary to reserve the correct number of seats for the faculty, to have the right robe for each man in the robing area assigned to him, to see that the programs are available both at the chapel doors and in the robing rooms, and to repack the robes and return them to the owners or to the rental service afterwards. The chaplain's office usually orders the flowers for the altar and the chancel, and assembles and delivers the material for the program to the printers.

As noted above, private services such as weddings, baptisms, and funerals take place in the university chapel throughout the year, and are the province and responsibility of the chaplains. There was one time at Columbia, however, when we of the Secretary's office became involved. A professor on campus who was an avowed atheist had died, and some of his colleagues and students wanted to hold a memorial service. They would have no part of the chapel nor of the assembly rooms in the religion building on campus. "No religious trappings whatsoever," was the edict. Someone thought of our Faculty Room, which is in Low Memorial Library, and representatives of the family of the deceased and of his colleagues looked the room over and agreed it would be suitable—although the room houses a fine collection of Chinese art, the dominating feature of which is a huge head of Buddha, with smaller statues of buddhas in the niches of the windows. Apparently the proviso against "religious trappings" applied no farther East than the Euphrates.

BACCALAUREATE SUNDAY

Baccalaureate Sunday is essentially a church service for the benefit of the undergraduate degree candidates, and takes place the Sunday immediately preceding commencement. It may be the only time that the chaplain reaches many of these young people, and he usually delivers a thoughtful and moving sermon. During Dr. John Krumm's tenure at Columbia, seniors, as they left this service, have been heard to say, "I wish I had gotten to know that man while I was a student"—which is a sad commentary on present-day pressures at a university.

Since the preparations for the Baccalaureate service are inextricably bound up with those for commencement, the details involved will be discussed in chapter 6.

5 CONVOCATIONS

SOME INSTITUTIONS hold a convocation at the beginning of each school year which is attended by the faculty in academic dress and at which the President delivers a "State of the College" address. At many other institutions a convocation serves as a small-scale commencement, for the purpose of awarding one or more honorary degrees to persons of distinction. It may mark a special anniversary for a segment of a university, or it may be held because someone particularly eminent, to whom the institution has long wanted to give a degree, is coming to the area but cannot attend the regular commencement. This sort of convocation is the subject of this chapter.

A description of the work entailed can best be dealt with in several sections: arrangements for the candidate; printing orders; faculty involvement; organization of the ceremony; and social entertaining connected with the event.

ARRANGEMENTS FOR THE CANDIDATE

The decision to confer an honorary degree is made by the trustees or governing board of the institution, to whom the name of a candidate is presented by the President. When approval has been granted, a letter from the President offering the degree and setting the date goes out. Follow-up upon acceptance is made by the Secretary of the university, as in the case of a visiting lecturer, except that in addition to asking when the candidate will arrive, whether he plans to bring his wife, where he wishes to stay, whether he wishes his transportation arranged, his personal guest list for the ceremony, and so forth, the Secretary must also obtain as soon as possible the candidate's hat and suit sizes as well as his height so that academic dress can be ordered for him.

At Columbia, as at most universities, a candidate for an honorary degree is expected to pay for his own travel, but his accommodations for the few days of ceremonies are provided by the university and he is given academic dress made to order for him. The latter practice may be due to the fact that Columbia has a distinctive robe of slate gray instead of the usual black, and a velvet tam instead of the stiff mortar board. (The hood is also a different shape from the usual.) At some institutions only the hood is given the candidate, and if he is bringing no robe of his own, one is rented for him.

In any case, as soon as the information has been received from the candidate, it is necessary to make all reservations, and order his robe from the tailor and his diploma from the registrar's office. This had better be done promptly since so many other people are involved. There may be a lengthy and elaborate process approximating copper-plate script involved in the preparation of the diploma, for instance.

PRINTING ORDERS

The printing necessary for a convocation involves the invitations to the ceremony, reply cards and envelopes to be included with the invitations, tickets to be mailed to those responding affirmatively, envelopes in which to mail the tickets, and an attractive souvenir program to be given out at the ceremony. (Also, of course, if there is to be a reception, dinner, luncheon, or tea before or after the ceremony in honor of the candidate, printing orders should be given for the invitations at the same time.)

The invitation is issued in the name of the trustees and the President and should bear the seal of the university embossed on the best vellum paper. The invitation should read as follows:

THE PRESIDENT AND TRUSTEES

OF

IVY UNIVERSITY

REQUEST THE HONOR OF YOUR PRESENCE

AT A UNIVERSITY CONVOCATION

TO HONOR

HIS EXCELLENCY THE PREMIER OF ATLANTIS

MONDAY, NOVEMBER TWENTY-FOURTH

NINETEEN HUNDRED AND SIXTY-NINE

AT FOUR IN THE AFTERNOON

THE GREAT HALL, SMITH LIBRARY

Please reply on　　　　　　　　　　　*Cards of admission*
the enclosed card　　　　　　　　　　*will be sent*
　　　　　　　　　　　　　　　　　　　upon acceptance

Sometimes the name of the candidate does not appear on the invitation face, provided a descriptive phrase can be used instead, or in cases where the event (the hundredth anniversary of a school, for instance) overshadows the eminence of the candidate, or when several candidates are involved. Some while ago, on the occasion of the hundredth anniversary of the founding of the School of Engineering at Columbia, three degrees were conferred. On the first page of the invitation was ". . . at a University convocation to honor three distinguished engineers on the occasion of the hundredth anniversary of the founding of the School of Engineering." On the inside of the fold (third page) the three men were named.

The reply card to be enclosed with the invitation bears the usual wording:

Please send_____tickets for the
University convocation on Monday,
November 24, 1969, in the Great Hall,
Smith Library, Ivy University.

Name_____
(please print)

Address_____ Zip code_____

The ticket should read:

IVY UNIVERSITY CONVOCATION
NOVEMBER 24, 1969, AT 4:00 P.M.
THE GREAT HALL, SMITH LIBRARY
(*Guests must be seated before 3:55 P.M.*)

The latter admonition is included so that the arriving guests will not be in the way of the assembling academic procession.

The program, which need not be printed as early as the invitations, since it will not be used until the day of the ceremony is composed of a number of pages. It gives the order of the ceremony, the words of the anthem sung by the choir (if the choir participates), and usually the words of the institution's Alma Mater with which the ceremony is closed. The various components of the ceremony will be discussed in detail when outlining the copy to be given the printer for the program.

While the printing of the invitations is going on, the list of invitees must be assembled. If the convocation is to honor a particular school within the university or to mark an anniversary of some sort, the guest list must include persons intimately connected with that segment of the institution: alumni, donors, and distinguished faculty—past and present. It also includes persons of neighboring institutions, from their presidents to those on their faculties who have distinguished themselves in the particular field; local and state officials of government and, indeed, federal as well, if the person to be honored is an official of another nation. At Columbia we always invite the appropriate ambassadors to the U.N. Those institutions outside New York probably would not do so, but the consul of the candidate's country stationed nearest should be invited, as well as his ambassador to Washington.

If the degree candidate is a member of the clergy, the leading churchmen of all faiths in the immediate area should be invited, as well as his overseer, whatever his title or place of residence. For instance, when Columbia gave an honorary degree to the Archbishop of Canterbury, invitations were sent to Her Majesty Queen Elizabeth as his immediate superior and to her ambassadors to the United States and to the UN, and of course to the leading bishops of the Episcopal Church in America, as well as to church leaders of other faiths resident in New York City.

The examples above are given to point out that the invitation list for a convocation must be carefully compiled to fit the occasion and the candidate. There will always be a list of a certain group who are invited to everything, which list should be in an index file readily available. From time to time this will need revising and should be examined at least every six months to be kept up to date. At this time it is imperative to include the candidate's personal list among those to whom the invitations will be sent.

The replies from the invitations will come in just when other preparations are at their peak. There must be no delay in sending out the tickets. If possible some temporary help to handle them should be engaged. Nothing can breed ill-will faster than careless or slow handling of ticket requests.

FACULTY INVOLVEMENT

A convocation, being a junior-sized commencement, generally involves the faculty, or part of it, in the academic

procession opening the ceremony. For instance, for the convocation which conferred degrees on three distinguished engineers in honor of the Engineering School's anniversary, there were more than fifty members of the engineering faculty in the procession, three faculty members as escorts for the candidates, the deans of the School, the chairman of public ceremonies (master of ceremonies is his function), the chaplain, the mace bearer, and the President. Two marshals chosen from the faculty (they are often assistant deans) are responsible for lining up their colleagues according to seniority, and one marshal at least is in charge of the student ushers. Several marshals are appointed to escort the wives of the candidates and the dais party members to their special seats, much as the way the mothers of the bride and groom at a wedding are escorted to their places just before the ceremony begins.

One of the first things to do, therefore, is to find out how many faculty members will be involved in the ceremony, and to order their academic dress if they do not own it. The order form appears on the following page.

ORGANIZATION OF THE CEREMONY

An important segment of a convocation is the *music*. At Columbia the processional and recessional music is played by a brass choir stationed in the balcony overlooking the Rotunda. The music used was specially composed by Otto Luening and takes full advantage of the resonances of the Rotunda. If other institutions do not have such a place for formal ceremonies, or a comparable composer in residence,

ACADEMIC DRESS REQUEST FORM

Name _____

Office Address _____

Telephone _____

Occasion _____

    Height _____   Cap _____

    Weight _____   Gown _____

    Hat Size _____   Hood _____

    Chest Measurement _____   _____

    Suit Size _____   _____

    Highest Degree _____   Institution _____

Note: For office use only; do not write below this line

‒ ‒ ‒ ‒ ‒ ‒ ‒ ‒ ‒ ‒ ‒ ‒ ‒ ‒ ‒

    Date Borrowed _____

    Date Returned _____   To be mailed _____

    Date Necessary _____   To be picked up ___

live music is still much to be preferred to a taped or recorded version of "Pomp and Circumstance." As well as the brass ensemble, the chapel choir usually takes part in the ceremony, singing one anthem (a cappella) and the Alma Mater at the conclusion. Arrangements must be made early in the preparations for both the musicians and the choir. Be sure to ask the choir director for the words of the anthem he plans to conduct so that they can appear in the program.

If the degree candidate is a head of state or an official of another country, the national anthem of that country should also be sung, followed by the "Star Spangled Banner." The foreign anthem may pose a problem for the choir, especially if the nation so honored has an unfamiliar language, but if at all possible the choir should sing it—phonetically if necessary. Such a gracious gesture is a compliment to the candidate and his fellow countrymen in the audience, so should not be overlooked.

Well in advance of the convocation, instructions should go out to the escort or escorts of candidates as well as to the other members of the dais group. It is well to lay out a step-by-step choreography—who marches with whom and where each sits, as well as the part to be played by each of the principals during the ceremony. Here is the instruction sheet used at a recent ceremony. It is somewhat simpler than most because the choir did not appear at this convocation (it took place so early in the school year that the choir members had not arrived on campus). Had the choir participated they would have lead the procession and ended the recession.

CONVOCATION
Fiftieth Anniversary
Graduate School of Business
Thursday, September 22, 1966

INSTRUCTIONS FOR CANDIDATES, ESCORTS,
AND THE PRESIDENT'S GROUP

Assembly: Members of the dais group and the trustees will assemble at 4:00 P.M. in the Trustees Room, 212 Low Memorial Library.

Members of the Faculty of the School of Business will assemble in the southwest corridor at the 100 level of Low Library at 4:10 under the direction of Marshals Pontecorvo and Berg.

Academic Dress: Academic robes for the dais group and the trustees will be found in the cloakroom of the Trustees Room. Members of the Secretary's staff will be present to assist in robing and to receive academic gowns after the ceremony.

OUTLINE FOR THE CEREMONY

The Academic Procession will consist of the Faculty of the School of Business, the trustees, and the dais group. At about 4:20, on signal from Mr. Graham of the Secretary's office, Marshals Pontecorvo and Berg will lead the faculty in a double line up the southwest steps to the head of the middle aisle of the Rotunda.

At 4:30 as the music for the Processional begins, Marshals Berg and Pontecorvo will lead the faculty procession down the center aisle to the first row of seats on the left. The marshals will direct the seating of the faculty and of the trustees, who will follow immediately after the faculty and sit in the front row on the left side of the aisle.

The dais party will form in line as follows:

Chaplain Cannon	Mr. McMenamin
Professor Smith	Mr. Sporn
Professor Burns	Sir Jehangir Ghandy
Professor Benoit	Mr. Eyskens

Dean Brown
Professor Devons, Mace Bearer
The President

The dais group will follow the faculty and trustees and, on arriving at the dais, will turn right or left as indicated on the attached diagram and move to their designated seats.

Faculty, trustees, and the dais group will remain standing until the President takes his seat.

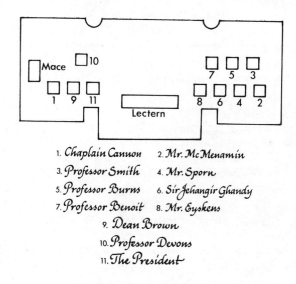

1. *Chaplain Cannon* 2. *Mr. McMenamin*
3. *Professor Smith* 4. *Mr. Sporn*
5. *Professor Burns* 6. *Sir Jehangir Ghandy*
7. *Professor Benoit* 8. *Mr. Eyskens*
9. *Dean Brown*
10. *Professor Devons*
11. *The President*

THE CEREMONY

1. Mr. McMenamin will request the permission of the President to begin the ceremony.
2. Mr. McMenamin will present Chaplain Cannon who will deliver the Invocation.
3. Mr. McMenamin will introduce Dean Brown and the President.
4. The procedure for each award will be as follows:
   a. Dean Brown, after his opening remarks, will present each candidate in the program order. When he says, "Mr. President I have the honor to present ——————," The President will rise and stand at the lectern. The

candidate and his escort will rise, the candidate placing his cap on his chair, the escort carrying the hood. The candidate will approach the lectern and the escort will take a position behind him.

b. The President will read the citation and immediately after present the diploma. The escort will place the hood over the candidate's shoulders.

c. The candidate and escort return to their seats, the candidate resuming his cap.

d. The same procedure will be followed for each of the other degree recipients. The President and Dean Brown will then resume their seats.

5. Mr. McMenamin will present Sir Jehangir Ghandy to respond for the degree recipients.

6. On the conclusion of Sir Jehangir's address, Mr. McMenamin will present Chaplain Cannon to pronounce the Benediction. All will remain standing for the Benediction.

As the music for the Recessional begins, the dais party will lead the Recession followed by the trustees and the faculty. The dais party will return in inverse order to that of the Procession led by the mace bearer, Professor Devons.

ORDER OF RECESSIONAL

Chaplain Cannon	Mr. McMenamin
Professor Smith	Mr. Sporn
Professor Burns	Sir Jehangir Ghandy
Professor Benoit	Mr. Eyskens

Dean Brown
The President
Professor Devons, Mace Bearer

Trustees' Instructions: Your robes will be in the Trustees' cloakroom. Please assemble by 4:10 if possible. You will march after the faculty and before the dais group to seats in the front row left. In the recessional you will follow immediately after the dais party and before the faculty.

Faculty Instructions: Please assemble in the first floor corridor, southwest area of Low Library at 4:10 p.m. If you have ordered academic robes from the Secretary's Office, they will be available at the assembly place. If you have not ordered, please bring appropriate robes.

Marshals' Instructions: Please report to the faculty assembly area by 4:05. After members are robed, please arrange the procession in a column of two abreast in order of seniority. A list of the proper order will be furnished to you. At 4:20, on a signal from Mr. Graham of the Secretary's Office, you will lead the column up the southwest stairs to the head of the middle aisle of the Rotunda. You will stop there until a signal from Mr. Graham to enter the Rotunda. The three front rows of seats on the left will be reserved for your group. Fill the *third* row first, then the second, then the first. The trustees should be seated in the first row. Reserve the aisle seat in the second and third rows for yourselves.

After the Benediction, the marshals will stand in front of the fourth row on each side (occupied by guests) while the dais party leaves, followed by your group in reverse order (front row first, then second, then third). The marshals will follow the last rank of faculty from the Rotunda.

The program used for the same convocation follows. If the choir had participated, it would have sung an anthem after the Invocation and before the Presentation of Candidates, and the words of the anthem would have been included, as well as credit for the choir director. Then again, after the Response would have appeared Columbia's Alma Mater, with a small notice under it stating that the words

[*front cover*]

COLUMBIA UNIVERSITY
IN THE CITY OF NEW YORK
[*seal*]
UNIVERSITY CONVOCATION
IN COMMEMORATION OF
THE FIFTIETH ANNIVERSARY
OF
THE FOUNDING OF
THE COLUMBIA BUSINESS SCHOOL

THURSDAY, SEPTEMBER 22, 1966
FOUR-THIRTY O'CLOCK IN THE AFTERNOON
THE ROTUNDA, LOW MEMORIAL LIBRARY

[*left-hand page*]   *Processional*
PROCESSIONAL MUSIC
by
The Columbia University Brass Ensemble
under the direction of Elias Dann

Invocation
JOHN D. CANNON
Chaplain of the University

Presentation of Candidates
COURTNEY C. BROWN
Dean of the Graduate School of Business

[*right-hand page*]   *Conferring of*
the Degree of Doctor of Laws
THE PRESIDENT OF THE UNIVERSITY
Gaston Eyskens
Sir Jehangir Jivaji Ghandy
Philip Sporn

Response
SIR JEHANGIR JIVAJI GHANDY

Benediction

Recessional

were on the last page. (We never print the words of the National Anthem, although not many more people seem to know them than know "Stand, Columbia!")

Preparations for the ceremony must include the physical preparation of the auditorium, and so orders must go out to Buildings and Grounds for the requisite number of seats in the auditorium, chairs on the dais (preferably with a diagram of their arrangement), sound system, chairs and music stands for the musicians, and water and glasses by the lectern. The head of the Security Guard should be notified, and he will want to make special arrangements if your institution is honoring a foreign dignitary. The audio department will need to tape the proceedings and monitor the sound system.

Let me counsel once more that it is all better accomplished with a good check list. Some may prefer to have a master check list made up in quantity which covers any sort of academic occasion, rather than one for receptions, one for dinners, one for lectures, one for convocations, and so forth. A sample comprehensive check list appears in the Appendix.

SOCIAL EVENTS

There is invariably some social entertaining of the guest or guests of honor, which take the form of one of the occasions previously described: either a reception following the awarding of the degree, a dinner either the night before or the night of the ceremony, or a luncheon preceding it. Sometimes the honored guest is asked to remain on campus for a day or two for a colloquium with outstanding students in his field. In such a case arrangements must be made for small lunches and dinners while he is there. Someone may also have to be tapped to take him to breakfast, but only if he is the garrulous and hearty type who likes company early in the morning. (I don't know how you'll tell what he's like until you meet him. Better to leave him in peace than not.) In any case, the chairman of the department or the dean of the school concerned will undoubtedly do the honors and you need only stand by to make reservations and so on. It is over as far as you are concerned, except to collect the automatic letters of thanks for doing a job you were hired to do in the first place.

6　COMMENCEMENT

THE ANNUAL COMMENCEMENT exercise is the high point of the academic calendar, no matter whether the institution is large or small. The purpose, after all, of any college or university is to prepare its student body to merit academic degrees. Commencement is the recognition of its success, and that of its students, in the undertaking. Therefore, the President (or Chancellor, Rector, or whatever he is called), because he personifies the university, is the star of the ceremony.

The exercises can be elaborate and formal, or simple and informal. Harvard's commencement is probably the most ritualistic, as befits the oldest college in the United States. There tradition looms large, with the Governor of the Commonwealth arriving escorted by troopers on horseback, pennants held aloft, and the sheriff of the county opening the exercises by announcing the "meeting" is convened. (At Harvard the Board of Governors assemble and march to the platform wearing formal morning clothes and silk hats.) By contrast the commencement exercise in a small college in the Kentucky mountains is almost a family reunion, with the relatives of the graduating class sitting on the grass wherever they choose and enjoying a picnic lunch during the ceremony.

The majority of commencement programs fall somewhere between the two cases cited above. One thing most of them have in common is the holding of the exercises out of doors. This not only adds to the festive air but makes it possible for many more people to attend than could be seated in any auditorium. (It means, however, that a carefully planned rain program must be developed along with that for the outdoor ceremony; see page 84.)

Any commencement plan involves many departments. At Columbia some of them are: University Relations, alumni offices, the Registrar's office, Buildings and Grounds, Security, the campus ticket office, the chaplain's office, and that of each dean of a school or faculty, to say nothing of the President's staff and the President's lady. At each orderly commencement there must be an overall head of the enterprise, the producer of the spectacle, through whom all information and plans must be cleared. Such an officer is directly responsible to the President, and preliminary work begins about the middle of February.

Before discussing preparations in chronological order, a brief description of the various *dramatis personnae* who usually take part in commencement exercises may be helpful.

Marshals (or ushers if you will) are usually younger faculty members who wear their academic gowns, and aiguillettes for identification. (An aiguillette is the loop of rope in a bright color, complete with tassels, worn over the left shoulder and arm. It used to be worn by doormen in front of large motion picture and apartment houses. In academic circles it merely means "an official.") On small campuses in rural communities marshals may be unnecessary; but at larger academic communities, particularly in cities, marshals are needed to help control traffic on campus, and to direct the guests to the seating area to which their tickets entitle them. They also organize the various sections of the academic procession.

Hood marshals are part of the dais party, and their function is to put the academic hood on each honorary degree candidate as the President reads the citation and hands him his diploma. (If there are to be twelve honorary degree candidates, they usually sit six on each side of the platform. This necessitates four hood marshals, two on each side, to place the hood on the candidate as the President finishes conferring the degree. It is not unlike Western roping and requires some practice to perform smoothly.) If, as at some institutions, two hood marshals are appointed, one each from the twenty-fifth and fiftieth reunion classes, there should be two experienced faculty members to assist them.

Honorary degree candidates, although not a necessary part of any commencement, are the rule on most campuses rather than the exception. The same procedures obtain as those followed for the candidates honored at a convocation. If a college or university does not award honorary degrees at its commencement exercises, it probably has a "guest speaker" of national or regional importance. The courtesies described both in the convocation section and in the following apply to such a guest, whether he is to receive a degree or not.

Escorts for honorary degree candidates are members of the faculty who have some eminence in the fields of the particular men to whom they are assigned. For instance, a candidate who is an industrialist is likely to have as escort a senior member of the faculty of the School of Business; and a foreign diplomat, someone from the School of International Affairs. A head of state would be escorted by the dean of the school in which his interests lie. An escort is responsible for meeting his particular candidate when he arrives in the city or town of the institution, accompanying him to the campus and to all social functions connected with commencement, as well as bringing him to the assembly point for the exercises, seeing that he is made comfortable at all times—in other words, acting as a host to the distinguished visitor.

Alumni office personnel have considerable responsibility on most campuses for commencement. At some institutions reunions of nearly every class below the twentieth occur, and plans must be made for their housing, feeding, entertainment, instruction, and so forth. On Ivy League campuses there is a growing involvement of the reunion classes. Years ago they used to return to recapture their youth in rather uproarious and uninhibited fashion. Now, by and large, they come back for more meaty stimulus. On many campuses there are available to the "old grads" seminars, lectures, and round-table discussions in many academic fields. They are well attended by both the alumni and their wives.

When alumni become the concern of the central commencement planning office it is because they are marching in the academic procession. At a large university it would be impossible to have all of the returning graduates in the procession. In such a case, they are given seats in a special section. If the campus is small or new, the number of alumni present may be small enough to allow them to become part of the procession. In any case they wear street clothes rather than academic robes.

The mace bearer, who carries a mace in the procession immediately preceding the President both entering and leaving the ceremony, is not found in the majority of exercises, but does exist on the older campuses in the East. The office of mace bearer is purely ceremonial, and derives from medieval times in England when an official—say the Lord of the Admiralty or the Chief Justice of the Court of Assizes —was taking office or opening his court and needed a bodyguard. Then the mace, a formidable weapon, was held ready to protect the person of the dignitary. From the sixteenth century in England and since colonial days in America, it has become a symbol of office only, and is carried by a distinguished member of the faculty (preferably one who is entitled to wear a colorful academic gown).

Since most of the preparations for commencement exercises follow the procedures detailed elsewhere in this book, a chronological list of chores should be sufficient. What follows, except for the events of the day itself, is a giant check list with explanations appended when the procedure is peculiar to commencements only. (N.B. There will be some items which can be ignored by many commencement impresarios; but it is my earnest hope that none is left out.)

1. The first step (taken in February at Columbia) in getting commencement under way is the letter of notification, giving the date and time of commencement, which is sent to the following:

The master of ceremonies (if he is other than the Vice-President or other important administrator)

The head chaplain

The mace bearer

The company which installs the sound system

The director of the building from which the procession will march

All of the campus service departments involved in the ceremony

The head of the alumni office. He is also asked to have the two hood marshals chosen, one each from the twenty-fifth and fiftieth anniversary classes. (When these marshals are named, they must be sent instructions and asked for their clothing sizes so that their academic dress can be ordered from the rental company.)

2. All of the faculty members who will act as marshals must be recruited. If there are several seating sections, there should be two marshals for each. There must be two marshals on each entrance to the campus and at least two marshals for each division of the academic procession.

3. When the proposed honorary degree candidates have indicated their acceptance to the President, the administration official in charge of commencement writes them for the same information he requests before a convocation at which a degree or degrees will be conferred, i.e., date and time the candidate expects to arrive, whether he plans to bring his wife, where he plans to stay, whether he wishes his travel arranged, and a request for his "vital statistics" (height and hat and suit sizes), so that academic dress can be ordered made for him, and also for a glossy photograph for the news office's publicity purposes.

4. A confidential letter is sent to the following persons: deans, Provost, Alumni Federation president, and news office staff, giving them the names of the honorary candidates, the degree to be awarded each, their escorts, where they will be staying, and any other information that seems pertinent. This is marked "confidential" because the list of those to receive honors is kept as secret as possible and is not usually released to the press until the night before commencement.

5. The diplomas for the honorary degree candidates are ordered. (Each dean orders the diplomas for the earned degree candidates.)

6. As soon as possible, academic dress for the "honoraries" is ordered made.

7. Forms for rental of academic dress are sent to all marshals, escorts, and medal winners if they are to receive their medals at commencement proper. It is astonishing how few members of the faculty, except deans, own their own robes.

If they are to serve as marshals or escorts, the university generally picks up the tab, but year after year they have to pay more than a tenth of the cost of a new robe when renting each time they are in a procession. (Even the mathematics department hasn't figured out how uneconomical this is.)

8. The printing order for commencement is large and complicated, so it had better be tackled as early as possible. It includes:

Invitations to the exercise. These are usually rather stiff cards which can fit into a regular office envelope. They go to parents of the graduating classes, university officials, trustees, members of the advisory councils, former trustees, professors emeritus, the President's personal list, the invitation lists of the honorary degree candidates, and any state, local, or federal dignitaries the university policy in such matters would encompass.

Tickets. Three go to each graduate on most campuses, two to each faculty member who requests them. The rest are sent out in response to requests from invitees. If there are several thousand invitations mailed, there will need to be several seating sections with distinctive colored tickets. Therefore it is necessary to set up and maintain a carefully updated card file of all invitees. Each card is coded so that when a request for tickets arrives, the tickets for the appropriate section can be dispatched without delay. (It must be apparent that, with several thousands of invitations sent, several temporary helpers must be hired; otherwise chaos would ensue.)

Printed instructions to graduating students. They should
be told where to pick up their robes, where and when to
return them after the ceremony, and where to assemble
for the procession. On the same page, instructions can
also appear concerning Class Day, if that is a separate ceremony, and the Baccalaureate Service, which usually
takes place on the Sunday preceding commencement.
Also the rain program should be included if the instructions differ.

Printed instructions to others in the procession—faculty
members, anniversary class members, advisory councils, trustees, and other dignitaries. They usually robe
and proceed from a different area than the students and
are accorded more attention and courtesy (for instance,
people to help them robe) than are the B.A. candidates,
alas.

Invitations to social events connected with the exercises.
On small campuses, the President's house is often the scene
of a reception for the graduates and their parents immediately following the exercises. At a large university,
however, such a reception would be unmanageable, and
so the deans hold receptions for their graduates, and the
President's is confined to the honored guests, administrative officials, trustees, and so forth.

The commencement program. This is the last and probably the most difficult of all printing orders. Generally
this includes the Order of the Exercises, then a listing
of prizes, medals, and honors generally follows, with the
name and class of the recipient in each case. At a small col-

lege those to receive degrees are listed under the degree (Bachelor of Arts, Bachelor of Science, and so on) alphabetically. At large universities with several thousand graduates this becomes impossible. Usually a supplementary bulletin is printed over the summer listing graduates for the year and printing the major addresses delivered at commencement. The commencement program sometimes carries a short history of the institution, with a chronology of its development by schools.

Besides a large check list of the sort outlined above, it is well to make a chart of the services to be rendered to the honorary degree candidates. I have found it useful to put this on an ordinary file folder. Open the folder and rule columns and lines across both faces.

As can be seen on the following chart, a dinner is usually given in honor of these guests of the university on the eve of commencement. It is held generally at the President's house. The invitations to such a dinner can be on engraved cards, with the date and occasion filled in by hand (see sample on page 8). Those invited are, besides the guests of honor and their wives, some trustees and a few high administrative officials, and in the case of a foreign head of state being among the honorary degree candidates, his ambassador to the United States and an Under Secretary of State from Washington or former American ambassador to the guest's country.

On the day of commencement, if the exercises take place in the afternoon, sometimes luncheons are held. At Columbia, the President's lady gives a luncheon for the wives of

NAME					
MARITAL STATUS					
DEGREE					
ESCORT					
PHOTO REC'D					
GUEST LIST REC'D					
HOTEL					
DINNER					
LADIES' LUNCHEON (W)					
ALUMNI LUNCHEON (M)					
PRESIDENT'S RECEPTION					
ACADEMIC DRESS SIZES					
TRANSPORTATION					

the honored guests while their husbands go to a luncheon given by the Alumni Federation. From those two affairs, escorts must be provided to bring the guests to their respective assembly points for the exercises—the ladies to special seats, the gentlemen to their robing area.

BACCALAUREATE SUNDAY

While preparations are going forward for the commencement exercises plans must be completed for Baccalaureate Sunday. At most universities attendance by the students is not mandatory, but it is a solemn and beautiful service and those who do attend glean something worthwhile.

Because of the seating problem it is important to get a reliable count on who will attend, if possible. The graduating class is asked to assemble by schools in various parts of the campus, with a marshal in charge of each section. At the proper time the students (in cap and gown), following the choir, march by twos into the chapel and occupy the front rows of pews. They are followed by members of the faculty, then deans, trustees, and chaplains (as in the case of Commemoration Sunday described in Chapter 4). The remainder of the seats are occupied by families of the degree candidates, who are seated before the procession begins. As in the case of other academic ceremonies, a capable head marshal and well-instructed marshals are essential to the well-ordered procession. It is possible to avoid foul-ups, halts, and confusion, but that takes careful planning of the lines of march and meticulous care to have just the right number of seats available. Some day I hope to see a perfect one.

CLASS DAY

At the larger universities, student prizes are awarded at Class Day, the valedictorian and the class president address their colleagues, the dean makes a farewell address to the graduates, the band plays, and sometimes a chorus sings. If the institution is an ivy-planting or tree-planting one, this ceremony is incorporated. Such a Class Day is planned and carried out by the dean's office. If there are several undergraduate schools spread over the campus each one has its own ceremony. Whoever is in charge of the commencement exercise preparations very seldom has anything to do for the Class Day ceremonies.

ACADEMIC DRESS

The academic costume worn today originated in the universities of the Middle Ages, when a warm gown and hood were useful for scholar and cleric in unheated buildings. The distinctive gown served to set the student apart from his fellow citizens, hence the perennial controversy between "town and gown." Until after the Civil War, students at most American universities wore caps and gowns daily while in residence. These varied in design until they were standardized by the American Intercollegiate Commission in 1894. At that time it was decided that all robes would be black; bachelors' gowns to be made of worsted stuff with pointed sleeves; masters' gowns of silk with long closed sleeves; doctors' gowns of silk with longer sleeves, and faced with black velvet from hem to neck and back. They also carried three velvet bands around each sleeve above the elbow. Hoods were made of the same materials as the gowns, the length varying with the degree. Only the lining of the hood indicated the university by its colors. The border of the hood indicated the academic discipline in which the degree was earned.

In the last few years many universities have decided to return to a distinctive gown design. For instance, Columbia's is now slate gray. The doctoral gown, with facing of black velvet, now has sleeve bands in the color of the wearer's discipline. A Columbia crown is embroidered in slate gray on the black velvet facing at chest height. The mortarboard has been replaced with a soft black velvet tam with a gold tassel. The bachelors' and masters' gowns are an adaptation with no velvet trim and the old stiff mortarboard in slate gray. The new hood is bib-shaped. The hood displays the university colors as in the past, and the facing shows the standard degree colors.

Throughout the United States, there has been no change in the standard colors which represent the disciplines. The color facing the hood, whether it is black or colored, indicates the following:

White: arts and letters, including journalism
Scarlet: theology
Purple: law
Green: medicine
Dark blue: philosophy
Yellow: science
Brown: architecture and the fine arts
Pink: music
Lilac: dentistry
Orange: engineering
Olive: pharmacy

Light brown: business
Lemon yellow: library service
Light blue: education
Peacock blue: international affairs
Citron yellow: social work
It would be impossible to list the colors of hood linings
for all the colleges and universities in America, but here is a
short list of some that will be seen in most academic proces-
sions:
Harvard: crimson
Yale: dark blue
Cornell: cardinal with two white chevrons
Dartmouth: dark green
University of Chicago: maroon
Princeton: orange with black chevron
Massachusetts Institute of Technology: red with gray
    chevron
University of Pennsylvania: cardinal with navy chevron
University of California: gold with blue chevron
Columbia: light blue with white chevron
Color especially brightens the academic procession in the
European and South American robes. British gowns are
fairly conservative, most being black, but the bachelors'
and masters' gowns are edged with white fur, the doctors'
hoods are scarlet. Not so the Scots' robes, which are for some
disciplines bright scarlet wool faced with matching taffeta.
In France, the five major universities wear the same robe
for each degree. It is buttoned down the front with thirty or
forty small buttons, tied with a sash complete with rosette at

the joining, and the hood is an ascot trimmed with white fur, the number of rows tokening the degree. The color of the robes themselves are orange for Letters, purple for Science, red for Law, and crimson for Medicine. The French cap is best described as a chef's hat, or a formal silk hat worn upside down. Altogether impressive.

Spanish and Dutch universities provide a great deal of color in a procession, for some of them wear an Elizabethan ruff and cape, and large handsome tams. The most spectacular costume of all, however, is that of a lady graduate from a Spanish university. Her robe is knee-length, very full, with an empire waistline, and on her head she wears what can only be described as a Tiffany lampshade. It is made of ice-blue satin, inverted-bowl or umbrella-shaped, and from a topknot, row on row of tiny blue glass beads hang down to the edge of the bonnet. Even the university in South America which adds Indian feathers to its headdress in honor of the Incas cannot compete.

Of course the rental company from which robes are procured cannot come up with foreign gowns, but the firm from which the majority of New York City universities get their academic dress has even been known to produce the hoods of Trinity College in Dallas and the University of New Mexico without a moment's hesitation.

One important element of commencement is *music*. Wherever possible the college or university band should be used, but if that is not feasible it is important that someone from the music department choose the recorded or taped music for the procession, not only for quality but for length. It is necessary to have a reasonably accurate estimate of the time the procession takes to reach its seats. During the exercises, the choir or chorus should sing an anthem, the school Alma Mater, and the national anthem. At Columbia an outside contractor sets up loud speakers along the line of march and near the dais a few days before the ceremony. Since the main part of the procession marches about the equivalent of two blocks a large number of speakers have to be synchronized to avoid "feed back," and this would be beyond the competence of the campus audio department.

So much for the personnel, early preparation, and services connected with commencement. As the Big Day approaches, a close coordination with the President's staff is imperative. During the last week the acceptances to the dinners, luncheons, exercises, and receptions are correlated and sent to the President; his administrative assistant (or executive secretary) must be kept informed of all developments, and she in turn lets the entrepreneur know whatever she has learned from the participants which might mean last-minute changes, and which may have been communicated directly to the President. The President's staff works in high gear at this time, as does the coordinator's assistant. The most valuable assets each can have are an even temper and a willingness to work around the clock.

There is no way to confine the preparations for commencement to a nine-to-five schedule during the last week. Here are some of the chores which must be accomplished. The rented robes for the hood marshals and escorts must be received, checked, and tagged. The robes of the trustees which have been stored at the university must be similarly checked and tagged and those which need it, pressed. Those trustees who keep their robes elsewhere must be politely reminded, through their secretaries, to bring their academic dress with them. The newly made robes of the honorary degree candidates must also be checked and tagged. Some time during the week before commencement, ten or twelve attractive secretaries must be borrowed from various offices on campus to help with the robing of the dais party, and a time set aside to teach them the details of robing.

On the day or evening before commencement all of the robes of the dais group must be taken to the building in which the procession is to assemble. This means approximately fifty-five gowns, hoods, and caps, each previously tagged with the wearer's name. At least two or three garment racks will be necessary, and it simplifies the robing if the trustees' gowns are on one and the "honoraries' " and their escorts' on another. The robes of the chaplain, the mace bearer, master of ceremonies, Vice-President, Provost, and President are usually on a third.

It is worth while setting up chairs in pairs to correspond to the line of march, each chair tagged with a name. When the gentlemen are robed, they are asked to sit in these chairs until the call to march comes.

In another assembly space in the same building, a similar set-up must be established for the deans, with the additional "prop" of a scroll tied with ribbon the color of the discipline of each. The deans will use these in the ceremony, as will be explained later. These scrolls should be placed on the chairs marked with the deans' names.

If there is a third division of dignitaries, such as trustees of affiliated corporations and various groups of university associates, they assemble in still another room and chairs should be set up for them in the correct order of march to eliminate confusion.

Important! Always have a few extra robes, hoods, and caps on hand. There is inevitably one trustee (and often several) who appears without the robe he promised to bring, or who decides at the last minute to attend after declining earlier. (When in doubt, provide them all with doctors' robes and doctor of philosophy hoods of your own institution. None is so modest that he will decline to accept the honor.) Have ice water and glasses in the robing rooms, also safety pins, needle, and thread. A first-aid kit is a good idea as well.

On the morning of commencement the dais is carefully prepared, using a previously constructed blue print. Just as a stage is set for a play, the chairs and props are arranged. On each chair a card should be placed bearing the user's name clearly written. If there are twelve honorary degree candidates, twelve escorts, four hood marshals, five administrative heads, eighteen deans, and twenty-six trustees, this becomes a large undertaking. Also on the dais must be the diplomas for the honorary degree candidates in the order in which they will be awarded, and in each diploma must be placed the citation which the President will read before he awards the degree. The hoods must be in a convenient place also. The President's speech should be placed on the lectern.

A few minutes before the procession begins each section of the assemblage is lead into a specific place by its marshals. At a large university, the graduating classes (which may number in the thousands) are not part of the academic procession but feed into their assigned seats by twos from the side, as the choir does. The procession, led by the head marshal, marches up the main aisle in the following order:

Alumni anniversary classes
Assistants, instructors, lecturers, and associates
Faculty appointed to professorial rank (in order of seniority, newest members first)
Administrative and emeritus officers of the university
University Council (or Senate)
Deans
Candidates for honorary degrees and their escorts
Trustees of affiliated corporations and University Associates
Former trustees and trustees
The President's party
(Master of Ceremonies; Vice-President and Provost; Head Chaplain; Mace Bearer; President)

Usually only the last five groups sit on the dais; the others sit in a front section of the audience.

THE PROGRAM (ORDER OF EXERCISES)

Following is the program used by most large universities. (In small colleges, there can be more student participation, and each graduate comes to the platform to be given his diploma and to have his hand shaken by the President; sometimes the valedictorian makes his address to the graduating class here rather than at Class Day.)

THE NATIONAL ANTHEM

INVOCATION by the chaplain

AN ANTHEM, sung by the choir (the words of which are printed in the program)

ADDRESS BY THE PRESIDENT (or a guest speaker)

CONFERRING OF DEGREES IN COURSE. (The Dean of the Faculties or Provost introduces each dean, who rises with the scroll in his hand, and presents it to the President, announcing that it contains the names of those who have qualified for the degree of bachelor of whatever. The candidates in that particular discipline rise, remove their caps, and the President confers the degree upon them en masse. At Harvard, in the case of bachelors' degrees, the President says, "I welcome you to the company of educated men"; in the case of graduate degrees, he says, "I welcome you to the company of scholars.")

ALMA MATER, sung by choir (and any old grads who can remember the words)

AWARD OF MEDALS by the Vice-President of the university

CONFERRING OF HONORARY DEGREES, candidates presented by the Vice-President. (The President reads the citation while the candidate stands, head uncovered, beside him. Then he is given his diploma and the new hood is placed over his head by the two hood marshals.

He returns to his seat. The same procedure is followed for each.)

BENEDICTION, pronounced by the chaplain

RECESSIONAL

The return march is almost the reverse of the processional, except that it is led off by the mace bearer, who always immediately precedes the President. The dais, therefore, is emptied before the front-seated faculty depart. (It is necessary to insert at the end of the program a note to the effect that guests and graduates are requested to remain in their places until the academic procession has returned to its place of origin, whatever the name of the hall.)

Now all that is left to do is the clearing up. The members of the procession leave their robes in the robing room, and these must be sorted out and dispatched—some into boxes for the rental company, some to the owners' offices, and those belonging to the honorary degree candidates either boxed for them to take with them, or wrapped for shipping to their homes. Like a wedding, the preparation is long and involved and the ceremony mercifully brief. The recovery time is likely to be longer.

Some mention has been made of a *rain program*. It would be futile to outline such an alternate plan in detail as each institution's facilities and requirements are different. However, it would be the height of folly to ignore the need for an alternate program. These things should be done: a plan drawn up which shows where each segment of the exercises will assemble, how many of the audience can be accommodated in the building where the degrees will be awarded, which tickets will entitle the holder to a seat in which hall, and so forth. Most campuses do not have one hall large enough to seat all of those who wish to attend.

At Columbia, the ceremony takes place in the Cathedral of St. John the Divine, which seats about one-fourth of the invited guests but is far larger than the largest of Columbia's auditoriums and is only three blocks off campus. Five other halls on campus and another church in the area take most of the overflow. These buildings must all be wired for sound before commencement, and if necessary provided with chairs. (It is hoped that closed TV can be installed at not too great a cost in future years.) To minimize confusion, each ticket to the exercises gives the location of the alternate hall to which the holder should go in case of rain; the instructions to the faculty and students also carry instructions for the rain program; and the marshals and escorts are thoroughly briefed. Unhappily, all the paraphernalia which has been carefully set up in the robing rooms and on the dais must all be moved to rooms at the Cathedral. The last time this was necessary, the decision to move came only two hours before the ceremony.

Actually, a steady downpour all day is far better than threatening skies, as the decision to move is then never in doubt and there is the whole morning to effect the change to indoors. There is a story that once during Nicholas Murray Butler's tenure as President of Columbia the exercises were held out-of-doors on a very gray day. Just as the program got to the conferring of degrees it began to pour, so President Butler said, "I hereby confer degrees on all who have earned them" and ran for shelter. It was the shortest commencement on record.

7   *INAUGURATION CEREMONIES*

AS RECENTLY as 1960, American institutions of learning installed a new President—or Rector or Chancellor—on the average of every nine years. Now it seems that either the length of tenure is much shorter or there are so many new colleges and universities that the need for installation ceremonies is greatly increased. The latest report is that each year nearly three hundred and seventy-five new presidents are installed.

To begin with, the term "inauguration" is applied to the whole event and the social occasions surrounding it; the "installation" is the actual swearing-in (or anointing, so to speak), which is the heart of the ceremony. There is no one proper ceremony common to all such exercises. They can, and do, range from a simple handing over of the symbols of office during the commencement exercises to a full-fledged international convocation of educators and members of the learned societies.

The important first step is for a decision to be reached

(by the trustees or their equivalent, with advice from the financial officer) as to how much money should be set aside for the ceremony's costs, and this will determine how elaborate a pageant is feasible. Another factor is whether the eminence of the man or woman to be installed, or a capital funds drive, warrants putting on a great show. Generally when the President-elect has been Acting President for a period of time, the ceremony of installation is incorporated in commencement and the surrounding pomp is held to a minimum.

If the installation is to take place at a separate time from commencement, the next important step is to appoint someone of extraordinary competence to head the inauguration committee, and to help him choose his working group well. Some institutions even hire an outside organization to come in and "stage" the inauguration. This has an advantage in that none of the university personnel have to be relieved of their regular duties. On the other hand, an outsider cannot hope to assimilate the individual "style" of the institution and, without optimum efficiency, can be a disruptive force in the administrative offices—which are inevitably cramped.

Let us assume that the inauguration will be the responsibility of the university personnel, headed by a competent man. The committee, at a minimum, should consist of a chairman and four persons with the following responsibilities.

Invitations and programs
The installation ceremony

Social events before and after the installation
Public relations

Committees, as such, can be either a blessing or a curse. In foundations and some other nonprofit organizations, committee membership can become a way of life. One man may be a member of half a dozen committees, a delegate to eight regional or national or international conventions a year, on the board of three or four affiliated institutions, and a member of two or three subcommittees within the boards. Almost all of his time may thus be taken up with these activities. He spends it in airports, hotels, and meetingrooms talking to or being talked to by the same dozen or so men who are shunted around the meeting circuit.

In university circles there are a generous number of committees, but usually they meet on their own grounds and, due to the pressure of their other commitments, do not succumb to the way of life of the committee member described above. The academic "ad hoc" committee, however, often seems to be more active than the permanent sort, just as in Washington the subcommittee seems to be more important and to get more newspaper and TV coverage than the parent committee of which it is nominally a part.

INVITATIONS AND PROGRAMS

The inauguration committee will need to be functioning for at least six months before the event. The person in charge of invitations and programs begins his work at that time, and should be given a staff large enough to do the work efficiently.

His first concern is assembling the invitation list, which encompasses three general groups: the representatives of other institutions and the learned societies; the usual distinguished friends of the university and its officials; and alumni and student representatives. The first group will be expected to march in the academic procession, the second to attend the exercises and probably a reception or luncheon preceding or following the ceremony, and the last will include some for the procession and some not. It will be necessary to set up a mistake-proof file of names, with a code letter indicating what sort of invitations each has received, what he has replied, and so forth, of which there is more later.

There are several sources for the first group (representatives of other institutions and the learned societies). Much depends on the sort of inauguration that has been approved. If it is to be elaborate and magnificent, then invitations will be sent to the presidents of most of the four-year colleges and universities in the United States. If it is to be kept to a modest size, the Association of American Universities' list of members, or the membership of the institution's regional association of colleges, may suffice. If the institution has much commerce with foreign universities, or is one of the older universities in the country, invitations may be sent also to the heads of the leading universities of the world. The proper procedure, after a decision on the areas to be covered, is to settle down with some of the following books: H. M. R. Keyes, ed., *International Handbook of Universities* (Washington, American Council on Education, 1965; gives all but Great Britain and the United

States); *Universities of the World Outside of the U.S.A.*
(Washington, American Council on Education, 1950); and
Allan M. Cartter, ed., *American Universities and Colleges*
(Washington, American Council on Education, 1964). The
learned societies (as well as many colleges and universities)
can be found in *The World of Learning* (London, Europa,
1962).

When the invitation list is determined, the next step is to
design the invitation and its accompanying cards to fit the
various categories of invitees. Here is one form:

THE TRUSTEES AND FACULTY

OF

IVY UNIVERSITY

REQUEST THE HONOR OF YOUR PRESENCE

AT THE INAUGURATION OF

JOHN JOSEPH JOHNSON

AS PRESIDENT OF THE UNIVERSITY

ON WEDNESDAY AFTERNOON, OCTOBER THE TWENTY-SECOND

NINETEEN HUNDRED AND SIXTY-NINE

AT HALF AFTER THREE O'CLOCK

THE GREAT HALL

SMITH FINE ARTS CENTER

JONESVILLE, NEW YORK

Informal reception
following the ceremony
Founders' Hall

The addition of the reception invitation in the lower left-
hand corner is, of course, contingent upon everyone who is
invited to the ceremony being welcome at the reception.
The inviters (the trustees and faculty, as above), can be the

board of governors of a state university, the college and faculty, or simply the trustees.

In addition to the invitations, various cards must be printed to fit each category of guest. Here is an example of the card for the delegates of other institutions and the learned societies.

Name of institution or organization _____

_____

Year of founding _____
Delegate's name _____
Official title
  or position _____
Highest degree _____
Mailing address _____

_____
(City)   (State)   (Zip code)

(Representatives are expected to provide their academic costume. *Please return this card by October 5 at which time the official list of representatives will be compiled.*)

If there is to be a luncheon before or immediately after the ceremony, such an announcement can be added to the above card, in this manner:

Representatives are invited to the Inaugural luncheon in the East Dining Room of Smith Hall at one p.m.

Shall attend _____ Shall not attend _____
Accompanied by wife or husband: Yes _____ No _____

Those on the general invitation list will receive a card enclosed with the invitation which reads:

I shall _____ I shall not _____
Attend the inauguration of
Dr. John Joseph Johnson
as President of Ivy University

Please send one ____ two _____ tickets to:

Name _____
(please print)
Address _____
_____ Zip _____

The favor of a reply is requested by October 10

A third type of card is enclosed with the invitations sent to faculty members and student representatives.

I shall march in the academic procession on October 22d

Name _____
(please print)
Department _____ Title _____
I have academic dress _____
I wish to rent academic dress _____
    highest degree _____ height _____
    institution _____ hat size _____

(Dress, if rented, must be picked up on October 21 at the bookstore. The procession will assemble promptly at 3 P.M. in front of the Library.)

I wish one _____ two _____ tickets for my family

A reply envelope large enough to accommodate the reply card must be enclosed with each mailing. On the face of the envelope must be printed the address of either the inauguration committee chairman, or the committee member who has undertaken the invitation responsibilities.

Tickets and campus passes must be printed at the same time as the invitations and cards. If the institution is large and in a city, a pass must be sent to each person, delegate or faculty member, who is to march in the procession so that the marshals will let him through the bastions. Each pass should state clearly where the holder is to report and at what time. (If an outdoor ceremony is planned, an alternate rain program must be included.)

Tickets for the general audience, and for special guests, can be printed on different colors of stock so that if there is preferential seating the marshals can manage it smoothly.

If there is to be a reception, a luncheon, or dinner in connection with the inauguration, and the invitation list crosses party lines, then such an invitation (following the suggested invitations in the previous chapters) can be enclosed with the mailing, and an appropriate reply card also.

Compiling the final copy for the programs must wait until the list of delegates from other institutions and from the learned societies is complete. These names must be listed in the program, the oldest first, with the delegate's name and rank following, thus:

DELEGATES FROM OTHER COLLEGES AND UNIVERSITIES

1249 Oxford University
      John Bull Stonehenge,
      Bywater and Sotheby
      Professor of Byzantine
      and Modern Greek

1636 Harvard University
      Cabot Lowell Schmidlap,
      Trustee emeritus

Foreign and domestic institutions are mixed, the order being determined by the year of the founding. The same is true for the delegates from the learned societies.

Generally speaking, the program follows this order:

[*page 1*]   THE ACADEMIC PROCESSION

Order of March

STUDENT REPRESENTATIVES
DELEGATES FROM OTHER COLLEGES AND UNIVERSITIES
DELEGATES FROM LEARNED SOCIETIES
THE FACULTY OF IVY UNIVERSITY
THE UNIVERSITY COUNCIL
THE TRUSTEES OF IVY UNIVERSITY
THE OFFICIAL PARTY

[*pages 2, 3, 4*]

DELEGATES FROM OTHER COLLEGES
AND UNIVERSITIES

[These as described above. They may be listed in double column. Indeed, as there may be several hundred it is desirable to do so in order to keep the printing bill down.]

[*pages 5, 6*]
DELEGATES FROM LEARNED SOCIETIES

[*page 7*]   ORDER OF EXERCISES

Processional
[title of music and composer]

Invocation
PETER PAUL MATTHEWS, PH.D., S.T.D.
Chaplain, Ivy University

Anthem
[title of music and composer]
IVY UNIVERSITY CHOIR
Wolfgang Jones, Ph.D., Director

Addresses
ROBERT REDDY
Chairman of Student Council
SEYMOUR GAINES
President of the Alumni Federation
J. QUINCY FAHRENHEIT, PH.D.
[a distinguished professor of the same
discipline as that of the president-elect]

Presentation of the Charter and Keys *
RICHARD BANK MONEYBAGS
Chairman of the Trustees †

Inaugural Address
John Joseph Johnson, B.A., M.A., Ph.D.

Alma Mater: Ivy, Ivy, Hail to Thee
(audience is requested to stand for the
Alma Mater and the Benediction)

Benediction

Recessional

On the next pages of the program it is customary to list the
former presidents of the institution, ending with the name
of the present installee. This list is followed by the trustees

* Or whatever other symbol of office is traditional.
† In the case of a state university, this presentation would be made by the
governor of the state or chairman of the State Board of Education.

of the college, beginning with the chairman, and ending with trustees emeritus.

Sometimes there is a short history of the college on the last page, or it can follow the list of presidents and precede the list of trustees.

RECORD OF INVITATIONS

When the reply cards arrive, each must be checked against the master file. There should be a file card for each invitee. In the case of invitations to the presidents of colleges or societies, the name of the *institution* should be the one used for reference, rather than the individual to whom the invitation was originally addressed. Since there are hundreds of installations in this country alone each year, no head of a college or society can attend even a meaningful fraction of them without impairing his usefulness in his job. Therefore a delegate will in all likelihood be named to attend as his proxy. He or she is likely to be an administrative official, department chairman, former trustee, or distinguished alumnus residing in the area of the inviting institution.

When the reply card comes in naming the delegate, this name and all of the pertinent information must be typed on the file card. The delegate card itself must be transmitted to the committee member in charge of the installation ceremony, and any social acceptance card sent to the committee member in charge of luncheon, dinner, or reception.

The sample file card shown is for delegates. Faculty reply cards should be kept separate and have a section provided

for information from those who wish to rent robes (delegates bring their own).

```
CD *
Name: _____ Lunch    A__R__      Wife    ____
Address:_____ Dinner    __ __      Husband____
President:_____
                     2nd mailing: Pass_____ticket_____
    Delegate:_____ date mailed_____
    Title:_____
    Address: _____


    Information transmitted _____
                              (date)
```

* C D = college delegate. Another code designation is L S D (!)=
learned society delegate. A and R of course stand for "accept" or "regret."

THE INSTALLATION CEREMONY

The committee member in charge of the ceremony must
be kept informed of all acceptances for the procession. Not
only must he have an accurate count, but he must have the
all-important "date of founding," since the order of the
procession depends on it. He must plan the seating carefully so that there are enough places reserved for the
marchers but few empty seats.

The remainder of his preparations are essentially the
same as for commencement except that his marshals must
be carefully rehearsed in the matter of assembling the line
of delegates. If at all possible the delegates should be assembled where they can sit down in chairs labeled with their

institutions' names and arranged in the order of march. If this is not feasible then the marshals must be chosen for tact and cool heads, for there is bound to be a delegate—or several—who stops to talk to an old friend near the head of the line and will march in still talking instead of going to his correct place. This may seem like quibbling, but it is astonishing how many delegates jealously guard their institution's antiquity. If a representative from a new college founded in the twentieth century marches ahead of the man from a college founded in the eighteenth century, there may be "words."

The official party (that is, the persons who will take part in the ceremony) is also the responsibility of this particular committee member. Robes, hotel or other accommodations, transportation to and from the campus, and so forth, are his province. The robes of the faculty who wish to rent should also be cleared through his office, so when the reply cards from faculty are received they must be recorded on the master file card and then turned over to the ceremony committee for robe ordering. Student delegates (usually one from each class and a student speaker) will wear bachelors' gowns and caps (tassels on the right side) and no hoods.

When lining up the official party for the procession, the cast of characters, varying from one ceremony to the next, will determine who walks with whom. If the former President of the institution has died or gone on to his next post, or left the campus in a huff, having been fired, then the mace bearer (if there is one) walks before the chairman of trustees or governor or whoever is to confer the title on the

new man. In the recessional, the mace bearer walks directly
before the new President. Here is a possible line up:

(*front*)
Head Marshal

Marshal		Marshal
Student Speaker		Alumni Speaker
Faculty Speaker		Chaplain
Provost		President-elect

Mace Bearer
Retiring President
(if present)

Chairman of the Trustees
(or Governor of the State)

The recessional will more or less reverse the order, except it
is led by the mace bearer, followed by the new President,
chairman of the trustees, former President, and so forth.

The committee member in charge of the ceremony also
must see that the programs, which the invitation committee
has seen through the printers' hands, are distributed by
marshals when tickets are presented. He must also have a
supply reserved to answer the many requests for copies
which will come in after the ceremony is over.

SOCIAL EVENTS

The one extra duty for the social events chairman, which
is not included elsewhere in this book, is to compile and

have printed or otherwise reproduced a list of distinguished people who are attending the reception, luncheon, or dinner. If it is either of the latter, there must be two guest lists ready near the entrance to the room. One is an alphabetical list, showing the table at which each guest will sit, and the other is a list, by institution, of the guests. The latter will also be given out at a reception if it is a formal one limited to those who are delegates and the most distinguished friends of the college. If there is to be an informal reception to which everyone attending the installation exercises is bid, then no list at all need be compiled.

If there is to be a formal meal, then the members of the official party will be seated together at a head table, and the others disposed at the other tables in such a way that no one feels he is "beneath the salt." This is perhaps the most difficult job of all to do, but there is no way to guide the making of such a seating plan without access to the guest list. Wisdom, tact, and a knowledge of the personalities involved are the best aids.

PUBLIC RELATIONS

The committee member in charge of public relations will, it is hoped, be familiar with the institution's policies in the matter of publicity. To invite coverage by local and possibly state publications and communications media, a meeting should be held at least two weeks before the inauguration to give details and plans to the assignment editors or their representatives. At such a meeting, photographic coverage will be discussed, as well as the placement of platforms for TV cameras, the possible rain program, and a convenient time (with regard to media deadlines) when the new President can hold a press conference and when a copy of his inaugural address will be available.

If there is to be an address of any importance to the news media at the luncheon or dinner, a table should be reserved for the press and telephones made available near the banquet room for the use of those with an immediate deadline.

All such arrangements should be left to the person responsible for public relations for the institution year in and year out. In fact he should probably be the fourth committee member. In other words, it is *not* a good idea to appoint a man to the inaugural committee and give him this assignment if he has had no experience in the field. Press relations are difficult at best. Only a "pro" who is accepted by newsmen as one of their own can really get good coverage of an academic event.

8 PROPER DRESS FOR PUBLIC OCCASIONS

AT SOME TIME during the planning and preparation for one of the ceremonies described in the foregoing chapters, the question usually comes up: "What shall I wear?" This is a problem which confronts women almost exclusively, since men, at least until recently, have resigned themselves to a comfortable obscurity in the matter of clothes.

Time was, not many years ago, when a professor's wife had little choice of wardrobe for public occasions beyond a threadbare suit or a depressingly dreary chiffon. These she wore year after year as a badge of office in the select company of the Genteel Poor. In the last decade, however, things have changed for the better. The enormous growth in public support of higher learning has made it possible for university salaries to reach respectable if not affluent proportions. The professor's wife has a little money to spend on herself; and, perhaps of equal importance, she now has some good examples on campus to follow. The influx of public and private grants has lured into teaching a growing number of men from business and nonacademic professions, which adds to the faculty wives women with keener eyes for fashion and a greater appreciation of the importance of dressing well. Now the average faculty wife is no longer dowdy. In fact, she is often beautifully and smartly clothed, a matter of applying good intelligence to the problem and having a little money to spend.

It is difficult to advise in detail on women's clothes since proper dress will vary somewhat from campus to campus according to climate and custom. However here is a general chart, followed by some "do's" and "don't's" which reflect the author's personal observations and opinions.

EVENT	WHAT TO WEAR
Daytime meeting or informal luncheon	Tailored suit or tailored dress
Formal luncheon or tea	The above, or a "silk" dress; hat, if customary, and white gloves
Reception, cocktail party, or informal dinner	Black, figured, or lighter "silk" dress or suit; dress usually of simple lines but ornate material

Daytime Ceremonies: commencement, convocation, baccalaureate, etc.	The above choices with a feminine hat and gloves
Formal dinner	So-called dinner dress, either long or short, sleeved or not (see third point below)
Evening reception, ball, formal dance	Full-length evening gown, long white kid gloves optional

Men's dress. For the first four categories above, men (when not in academic robes) should wear a dark suit, white shirt, and conservative tie. For the last two, dinner clothes (tuxedo, dinner jacket, "black tie"). Alas, full dress ("tails" or "white tie"), the handsomest of men's wear and the correct attire for a ball, is seldom worn now, although perhaps it will be revived on campuses if affluence increases.

Here are some general precepts to consider.

First, if in doubt, *under*dress rather than *over*dress. A well-made tailored suit can be worn to a great many events if the accessories are carefully chosen. A pretty blouse, white gloves, and a hat with a bit of dash to it can do the trick. Even that old stand-by, a string of pearls, or an attractive lapel or shoulder pin can add the necessary festive appearance. Depending on the current style, it is often possible by acquiring one suit, a skirt, two blouses, and a sweater to ring many changes.

Second, do not buy a costume that is so "in" it will be "out" in a year or less. Pay more attention to line and becoming color than the latest quirk of fashion.

Third, know your own figure faults. If there is to be a formal dinner you may wear a dress that is street-length or floor-length. Either is correct, but one will look well on you and the other may not. The same goes for sleeves. If your upper arms are bulgy or emaciated, choose whenever possible a dress with sleeves; if your arms are pretty, show them.

Fourth, a few rules about jewelry and good taste. There is an old saying that one piece of jewelry is better than two, two are better than three, and more than three is a Christmas tree. In spite of jewelers' promotion of matched sets of costume jewelry, never wear them all at once (necklace, earrings, pin, and bracelet). Choose one or two to compliment the dress you're wearing, and save the others for another occasion. If you are lucky enough to own one piece of "real" jewelry, whether it is a pin or a ring or a pair of earrings, wear it in solitary splendor. In any case, never mix the real with the costume.

Fifth, the matter of hat or no hat for daytime events is something of a local option. On some campuses no one wears a hat to anything but a church service. On others, hats have assumed a great importance. If in doubt, a good rule is that any time you would wear white gloves you should also wear a hat. This includes commencement, a daytime convocation, a formal luncheon, an afternoon reception.

Sixth, avoid a conspicuous color if you must make one costume do for many occasions. Do not inspire the comment: "There's Mrs. Jones in her red dress *again!*" By the same token, do not load yourself with perfume so that you can be "recognized" from afar. Conspicuousness is a luxury only the very beautiful can afford, and they need use no props to attract attention.

I am sure that a great many of these comments and suggestions are unnecessary, but perhaps they will confirm the reader in her own opinions on the various subjects and therefore be of some value.

Appendix: *BUDGETS AND CHECK LIST*

IT WILL PROBABLY be noted that no discussion of costs for any event has been included in this book. This is not an oversight. To quote the costs at one institution as a guideline for all others would be useless. Instead it would be well to take the check list which follows and mark off those services needed for a specific event and ask each department to give an estimate, e.g., what Buildings and Grounds would charge to set up four hundred chairs, or what the audio-visual department would charge to tape a lecture. Hotels, caterers, robe rental companies, and so forth, will gladly give an estimate which is accurate and on which a budget can be based.

CHECK LIST FOR _____

Place _____

Date _____

Time _____

In charge _____

Done

1. Memorandum to Diploma Desk requesting diploma or certificate for awardee _____
2. Order honorarium check from the Controller   _____
3. Prepare file folder on occasion   _____
4. Order academic hoods (and robes) for honorary degree recipients   _____
5. Order medals for medal recipients   _____
6. Preparation of guest list
   Trustees
   Members of the University Council
   Chairmen of departments
   Senior administrators
   Deans and directors
   Faculty
   Columbia Associates
   Advisory committees
   Foreign students
   Outside organizations
   Widows in area
   Committees
   Friends of honored guests
7. Orders for printing
   a. Invitations
      Number _____
      Delivery date _____
      Mailing date _____   _____
   b. Envelopes
      Number _____
      Typed and addressographed _____
      Handwritten _____   _____
   c. Reply cards   _____
   d. Reply envelopes   _____

Done

   e. Programs
      Number
      First galley proof
      Delivery date   ———
   f. Posters
      Number
      Delivery date
      Permission to post   ———
   g. Tickets
      Number   ——— Reserved ——— Unreserved
      Delivery date   ———
8. Record of Mailing
   a. Carded on 3-by-5 file cards
   b. Recorded replies
   c. Tally   ——— Yes ——— No   ———
9. Publicity
   a. News Office   Press conference ———
   b. College newspaper
   c. Community Affairs calendar
   d. Flyers for students' boxes
   e. Posters   ———
10. Chaplain asked to officiate   ———
11. Obtain speaker for evening   ———
12. Recruiting
   a. Marshals
      Number
      Academic dress
      Time available
      Station   ———
   b. Escorts
      Number
      Academic dress

Done

Time available
Station   _____
  c. Student ushers
Number needed _____
Station
Report to _____
  d. Parking attendants
Number
Time available
Station   _____
  e. Announcer   _____
13. Engaging public address system
  a. Audio-Visual Department Head
  b. Campus radio station
  c. Outside (Professional sound company)
Date Ordered _____   _____
Lectern _____ table mike _____   _____
Time _____   _____
No. of mikes _____   _____
Tape recording ____   _____
14. Buildings and Grounds set-up
  a. Checking facilities in _____ Check room _____ Other
  b. Number of matrons _____
  c. On duty from _____ to ____
  d. _____ chairs on dais
  e. Rugs needed _____
  f. Flags _____
  g. Lights _____ in Hall _____ Outside
  h. Lectern _____
  i. Number of chairs on floor _____
  j. Doors open at _____   _____
15. Security

Done

a. Special guards
b. Stations _____
16. Choir participation
   a. Arrange seating
   b. Number
   c. Program _____ _____
17. Band participation
   a. Arrange seating
   b. Number
   c. Program _____ _____
18. Hired music
   a. Orchestra engaged _____
   b. Pieces _____
   c. Play from _____ to _____ _____
19. Open Faculty Room _____ Other room _____
20. Order flowers for dais _____
                      wife of honored guest _____
                      tables _____
   a. Caterer arranges
   b. Florist
   c. Delivery time _____
   d. Delivery place _____
21. Receiving line
22. Dinner party
   a. Date
   b. Invitations from _____ President _____ Sec'y
   c. List of guests
   d. Time
   e. Place
   f. Menu
   g. Liquors
   h. Chauffeur engaged

Done

23. Hotel arrangements _____
24. Travel arrangements (university pays _____) _____
25. Chauffeur engaged and on hand: time _____
                                                place _____
26. Reserve section
    a. Cards _____ Roped _____
    b. Number of seats _____ _____
27. Instructions to Marshals
                  Ushers
                  Parking attendants
                  Announcer
                  Escorts _____
28. Mace bearer _____
29. Guest book and pen _____
30. Special arrangements for caterer _____
31. Letters of thanks for all concerned in planning _____

DATE DUE

HIGHSMITH 45-220